The
Jamaican-Canadian
Association
(1962-2012)

The Jamaican-Canadian Association (1962-2012)

Portrait of a Community Organization
(Warts and all)

ROY G. WILLIAMS

Copyright © 2012 by Roy G. Williams.

CANADA ISBN 978-0-9878349-0-4

Library of Congress Control Number: 2011962930
ISBN: Hardcover   978-1-4691-3979-1
         Softcover   978-1-4691-3978-4
         Ebook   978-1-4691-3980-7

All rights reserved. No part of this book may be reproduced or transmitted in any form or by any means, electronic or mechanical, including photocopying, recording, or by any information storage and retrieval system, without permission in writing from the copyright owner.

This book was printed in the United States of America.

Williams, Roy G.
The Jamaican-Canadian Association (1962-2012):
Portrait of a Community Organization (Warts and all).
With Contributions by: Erma Collins, BA, M.Ed.
                          Kamala-Jean Gopie
                          Daphne Bailey, Eunice Graham, Pam Powell
                          InFocus—Reprint

Photography: Dr. Sylvanus Thompson
                Edgrant photography

Design: Tekno Printing & Graphics
Transcribing Services: Grace Williams

To order additional copies of this book, contact:
Xlibris Corporation
1-888-795-4274
www.Xlibris.com
Orders@Xlibris.com
109730

Contents

Preface 7
Overview: Toronto (Circa 1950's-1960's) 9

Part 1   The First Decade—1962-1970 15
Part 2   The Decade of the 1970's (1971-1980) 37
Part 3   The Decade of the 80's (1980-1990) 57
Part 4   The Decade of the 90's (1990-2000) 87
Part 5   The First Decade of the New Century (2000-2010) 99

SUB-SECTORS, ACTIVITIES, AFFILIATES AND SUB-GROUPS

The JCA Membership 129
The Jamaican-Canadian Association Community Centre 136
Financing the JCA Over the Years 139
Social and Community Service 142
Innovative Fundraising—The JCA Walkathon 149
Boonoonoonos Brunch At JCA: The Beginning 153
Golf At The Jamaican Canadian Association (JCA) 156
The Jamaican Canadian Association Women's Committee 161
The North York Seniors' Health Center Family Advisory Committee 171
The JCA Saturday Morning Tutorial And Heritage Program 173
The Jamaican Canadian (Toronto) Credit Union Limited 176
JCA Domino Club 180
The JCA Stalwarts 182
Benefactors 190
Reflections and Projections 192

Notes 203
Appendices 205
Bibliography 229

Preface

I had contemplated for some time the need for a book about the Jamaican-Canadian Association (JCA). Firstly, the Association is nearing 50 years of its existence. Secondly, organizations with a predominantly black membership tend not to last beyond one generation. Thirdly, written account of black organizations and the black experience tend not to be done. Fourthly, more recent members, officers, and employees of the Association have few clues about the Association's origins, values, traditions or accomplishments. Fifthly, many outside of the JCA may not be aware of the varied aspects and activities that take place at the JCA. Finally, it appeared that no one was about to do so.

For all of the above reasons and because most or all of the original members will have exhausted their lifetime allotment within the next ten to fifteen years, I assigned myself the task of penning this document. I am not a professional book writer; therefore, some may find shortcomings in its content and style. Some may even dispute the accuracy of some matters based on different perceptions and recollections. However, I have tried to present the information accurately and truthfully, hopefully with a minimum of personal bias.

The plan of the book is to trace the development of the Jamaican-Canadian Association (JCA) decade by decade and to focus upon the accomplishments under the respective presidents. Recognizing that the presidents' success is a function of the executive and other committees and to recognize their contribution, I have attempted to list their names in the Appendix. I describe sub-groups within the Association and activities conducted by the Association. I have attempted to identify dates when a particular activity was initiated and to give credit to the person or persons involved. I have also appended financial data for those inclined to evaluate using financial criteria. The Appendices contain information for further perusal.

I wish to thank all the people who assisted me in this effort by providing information, clippings, documents, interviews, photographs, and writing some sections, duly credited. I thank Mr. Karl Fuller and Ms Erma Collins who have taken the trouble to read and offer valuable comments and corrections to portions of the manuscript. I thank Dr. Sylvanus Thompson for making his extensive photo gallery available and Mr. Eddie Grant for providing the more historic photographs. I wish to thank Dr. Vincent Conville for his forethought in providing to the National Archives of Canada documents which I was able to retrieve, as they could not be found at the JCA. Most of all I thank Grace Williams, who halfway through the process decided I was not doing too well with the typing. She then took over the job and shepherded this project through many revisions and rearrangements. She also became the project manager and insisted on my sticking with the job by reducing the number of days off that I was inclined to take. In the final analysis, however, I take full responsibility for any mistakes, inaccuracies or shortcomings, and I hope despite any imperfections that this work will begin to fill the void about the Jamaican-Canadian Association. It is my project for the JCA's 50th Anniversary.

Overview

Toronto (Circa 1950's-1960's)

Toronto in the early 1950's and 1960's was referred to as "Toronto the Good." It was a predominantly WASP (White-Anglo-Saxon-Protestant) town with fundamentalist WASP rural Ontario values. Every commercial establishment closed promptly at 6:00 p.m. daily. Entertainment establishments—mainly taverns and pubs—were solidly closed by midnight. So that by that witching hour on Saturdays, everything ground to a deafening halt. Everywhere was locked down. Sunday was a Holy Day for everyone. No stores, no movies, no ball games—nothing after the weekly Saturday night "Hockey Night in Canada" game. People had to improvise in providing their own entertainment which contributed to the emergence of scheduled basement parties. Churches abounded; and on Sundays their pews were full of people who, dressed in their "Sunday Best", adhered almost exclusively to one or other brand of the Christian religion. Some claim that you could start a bowling ball rolling at the top of Yonge Street and it would roll all the way down to Lake Ontario without meeting one obstacle in its way.

The government in Ontario was big "C" Conservative it seems like forever. It was led by Premier Leslie Frost who held the office from 1949 until he resigned in 1961. He was then followed by a succession of similarly-minded conservatives—John Robarts, Bill Davis, Frank Miller and others. Frost, to his credit, introduced some socially progressive legislation.

Liquor (alcohol) was sold only by the Government of Ontario through its Liquor Control Board of Ontario (LCBO) outlets. The entire dispensing of liquor and who, when, and where liquor could be legally obtained and consumed was determined by the Ontario Government through the Liquor Licence Board of Ontario. To buy liquor at one of these stores you had to have a licence which indicated that you are legally permitted to buy liquor. This license required that you disclose all your vital personal information. You lined up, filled out a form with all the information together with the type and quantity of liquor you wished to buy. You then presented it to a LCBO clerk who would go into the back warehouse, find the liquor, take it to the cashier, who after taking your money, would place the liquor into a plain brown bag. You could now leave the store with your liquor. But be aware that you should not dare to open that bottle of liquor until you have entered inside your house. It is to be consumed only in secret, behind closed doors—not on your verandah, not on your lawn. And if an opened bottle of liquor or beer was found in your car by the police you would be in BIG, BIG trouble. Beer, similarly, was sold in Brewers Warehouse Stores using the same procedure as required for the liquor stores. In the pubs where one would go to have a beer, gender segregation prevailed. Separate drinking areas were provided for men and women. Women could not have a beer in the room reserved for men. Men however, could venture into the women's section. It was really old fashioned and antiquated.

Nothing happened in Toronto on weekends except that people went to church on Sundays. There was no place to go on a Saturday night, except to a tavern and they all closed at midnight. Where would one go dancing? If one wanted any kind of excitement one would have to head south to Buffalo or Niagara Falls across the United States border. Stores closed promptly at 6:00 p.m. daily. Gas stations closed at 7:00 p.m. Bars and cocktail lounges closed at 12:00 midnight. There was little or no nightlife and weekends were dull.

Sundays literally were REST DAYS. There was no Sunday Sports until the Blue Jays baseball team was formed in 1977. The Federal Lord's Day Act of 1907, which prohibited the conduct of any business on Sunday, was in full force. In 1950 Ontario passed the Lord's Day (Ontario) Act to authorize municipalities to permit public games and sports—except horse racing—between 1:30 pm and 6:00 pm on Sundays, providing this was approved by municipal electors in a referendum. In the 1960's the Ontario Act was amended to allow cultural and recreational activities and trade shows, scientific exhibition and horse racing, while removing the referendum requirement for municipal sports exemptions. In addition to the Lord's Day Act there was the Ontario Retail Business Hours Act (1975) which regulated the operating hours of retail establishments.

The enactment of the Charter of Rights and Freedoms in 1982 proved to be the death knell for the Federal Lord's Day Act which was struck down by the Supreme Court of Canada in 1985. This finally ushered in the liberalization of the society with individual and groups being free to enjoy a range of activities on Sundays. The weekends began to come alive without any detrimental effect to church attendance.

Rural Ontario could be described as the "Bible Belt." The society was Ultra Conservative and even the Liberals were small "c" conservatives. Churches abounded and the pews were full on Sundays.

Toronto was a relatively small town surrounded by a collection of smaller boroughs—East York, York, North York, Leaside, Etobicoke, Scarborough, and Swansea. Many of these were more rural than urban. Farms were in easy reach of the city. Travel from Toronto to the suburbs was a long and arduous task because bridges connecting them had not yet been built. There was no Leaside Bridge, for example, connecting Leaside and East York. The transportation system was disjointed and the Toronto streetcars and buses only took you to the then city limits. Eglinton Avenue East did not extend much beyond Bayview Avenue. You could not get on the other side of the Don River.

A Lilly-White Canada

Toronto's WASP population consisted primarily of English, Scottish and Irish preferred immigrants, their ancestors and forebears, who were early settlers and or post War II entrants to Canada. These were supplemented by successive waves of Northern European immigrants and displaced persons from Germany, Poland, Czechoslovakia, Austria and later Southern Europe—Italy, Portugal, Hungary and Greece following World War II. All of these were preferred immigrants in keeping with Canada's "Keep Canada White" immigration policy. As a consequence a black person who happened to arrive in Toronto in the 1950's and 1960's would rarely see another black person for days or even weeks. They were very few and widely scattered. Only after being here for a while would one find out where to look to find the occasional black person.

Canada's exclusionary immigration policy effectively prevented black people from entering this country in any numbers at that time. Black people from the West Indies in Toronto during this period consisted of a small number of students attending the various universities; a small number of nurses the first of whom, Beatrice Massop, arrived from Jamaica in 1953 following 14 months of advocacy on her behalf by Donald Moore and the Negro Citizenship Association[1]; and a small number of other women who came on the West Indian Domestic Workers Scheme[2] (which started in 1955) to fill serious labor shortages in these labor market sectors.

In the 50 years between 1900 and 1949 a total of only 5,431[3] West Indians were admitted into Canada and the total number of West Indians in Canada reported by the 1951 census was 3, 888. Presumably some of them had subsequently emigrated. This number was for all of Canada. The distribution in all Canadian urban centers would be very, very small. The largest numbers would be found in Toronto, followed by Montreal, Winnipeg, Calgary and Vancouver. A black person would therefore feel very lonely and isolated and would long for, and seek the company and comfort of like persons. There were few opportunities for such social contact other than at some churches, not all of which were welcoming. Their memberships were totally white and you would still be a lonesome stranger if someone did not step out and warmly welcome you. This was not always easy when you are being seen as an outsider or an intruder.

In addition to West Indians there were other blacks in Canada, small pockets of whom existed in the Maritimes, particularly in Nova Scotia where the "Maroons" arrived from Jamaica in 1796 and stayed to build the Citadel in Halifax. In Southern Ontario in towns like Dresden, Blenheim, Buxton and Chatham there were blacks who had come from the United States of America via the "Underground Railroad." Yes, there were native-born blacks and West Indian immigrant blacks but they were so few and scattered that they were literally "invisible." Most males would find employment in service industries as janitors and on the Canadian National and Canadian Pacific Railways as porters. The females found employment in the garment industry and as domestic workers in the homes of the wealthy.

Some of these blacks had purchased homes in Toronto and university students in Toronto would try to find accommodation with black families who lived in the area bounded by Dundas Street to the south, Dupont Street to the north, Bathurst Street to the west and Avenue Road to the east. An active grapevine kept students informed of these "safe" houses. Outside of these there was a high risk of doors being slammed in one's face as some white people did not rent to blacks. The less blatant racists would lie to you about the non availability of the advertised unit by telling you that it was already rented.

The Immigration Door Swings Slightly Ajar

In the 10 years between 1950, and 1959 a total of 10,682 West Indians were admitted to Canada. This was twice as many as were admitted in the previous 50 years. Things had begun to change, if ever so slightly. External and internal social and economic pressures were being exerted and tentative and measured responses were beginning to emerge, even if grudgingly so. But hold on, there was more to come. West Indians admitted to Canada in the next decade 1960-1969 totaled 46,030. That was more than four times the number admitted in the preceding 10 years. Things were just beginning to heat up because in the succeeding decade (1970-1979) the flood gates were opened and 159,216 West Indians were admitted to Canada.[4]

Table 1 and Chart 1 (Appendix 1) show the number of Caribbean people who migrated to Canada in the 21 years 1956 to 1976—a total of 159,711 with the peak occurring in 1974. This inflow, it must be noted, was skewed in favor of females as the country favored nurses, teachers, and domestic workers, quite unconcerned with its attendant social and psychological consequences. Table 2 in Appendix 2 show the number of Jamaican male and female immigrants who arrived in Canada during the years 1973 through to 1996 and their dispersion in Canada, primarily to Ontario (86%), Quebec (6.6%) and the rest of Canada 7.2 percent. Not only West Indians were now being admitted in large numbers but Indians, Pakistanis, Chinese, South and Southeast Asians, Africans, Central and South Americans and all others. What happened? Why the change?

Before, during, and following this upsurge in non-white immigration, the general climate was unwelcoming to non-whites, particularly blacks. There was subtle and not-so subtle discrimination and racial prejudice that manifested itself in the refusal to hire eminently qualified persons, the refusal to rent flats and apartments, the refusal of service in restaurants and other public places, the inordinate amount of unnecessary attention paid to black men by the police, and an education system that had difficulty adapting to non-white children.

When you watched television the image of a lilly white Canada was reinforced as there was no evidence that other than white persons could read the news or act in plays and sitcoms until Bill Cosby became Dr. Huxtable on the Cosby Show in the United States in 1984. Eaton's, Simpsons' and the Bay's department store catalogues never displayed a non-white male or female model or manequin. The entire market place presumably was deemed to be white.

Canada literally was cold, unwelcoming and lonely. It required unusual grit and fortitude for the arriving black immigrants to settle and survive. During the extended period from its inception in 1962, it was the Jamaican-Canadian Association that spoke to the redressing of grievances for individuals that were unfairly treated and the liberalization of laws, policies and attitudes within the larger society. The JCA became a philosophical partner to, a natural ally of, and ultimately the successor to the Negro Citizenship Association (NCA) led by Donald Moore. Moore and the NCA was a major advocate, primarily on immigration matters in the 1950's and 1960's and was personally responsible for opening the immigration door to nurses and for advocating on behalf of household workers in the Domestic Worker Scheme.

Some JCA originals

Cynthia Donaldson, Beryl Nugent, Bernice Bailey, Roy Williams, Amy Nelson, Daphne Bailey, Pam Powell and Raphaelita Walker

Part 1

The First Decade—1962-1970

PLANNING FOR INDEPENDENCE—1962

I do not recall exactly when it started. It must have been in the Spring of 1962, but some Jamaicans had been alerted to the imminent transition of Jamaica from colony to independent nation status that would occur on August 6, 1962. We were aware that there would be grand celebrations in Jamaica. Jamaicans in Toronto were excited and enthused but there was neither structure nor any mechanism around which to organize and manifest our new-found patriotism. There was no embassy. There was no consulate. We were on our own. We were scattered about the city. There was no bonding entity or any cohesiveness vehicle.

Esmund S. Ricketts

Along came Esmund S. Ricketts, a man at least in his late sixties or seventies. He was always dressed in a dark suit. He always wore an old felt hat. He always carried a black brief case and a black clarinet case. He lived on his own, and he always walked the streets of Toronto. He was a music teacher. He taught clarinet, piano and saxophone to predominantly black families and their children. As a consequence he seemed to know all the black families then living in Toronto. In the late 1950's and 1960's the black population was not large and most black people seemed to know or know of each other. They mostly attended the AME church on Soho Street or the BME church on Shaw Street. Ricketts was never reluctant to approach another black person to advocate for various groups relating to the Black experience be it the Marcus Garvey movement, the United Negro Improvement Association (UNIA), the United Negro Credit Union, and of course, the need to teach music to one's children and his willingness to aid in this endeavour.

Ricketts had served in the Second World War and he continued to maintain his military connections—especially with Lieut.-Col. B. J. Legge, QC, his mentor and legal counsel. He was part of a military band (I think the Royal Canadian Regiment band) and you could always count on seeing this lone black man in uniform marching in step with the much younger white soldiers playing his clarinet in the annual Santa Claus parades, other military parades, and annually at the Canadian National Exhibition. I cannot recall the circumstances by which we met, but I am sure that it was Ricketts who made the contact because he was not a shy man.

Ricketts, an ardent Garveyite, insisted that this historical event could not go uncelebrated. Questions immediately arose as to who, how, when, and where would this be done. He undertook to contact people and persuade them to come to a meeting. This was not an easy task as some people were skeptical and suspicious. They were skeptical of meetings. They were suspicious of strangers. Many in the Jamaican Community were new arrivals to Canada. They did not know each other and some were influenced by their attitude regarding class and status.

As to the question of where would the meeting take place, again Ricketts had a solution. The Home Service Association (HSA) building at 941 Bathurst Street was a meeting space provided by the City of Toronto for various black entities and programs such as glee clubs, choirs, and various meetings. It was also a casual meeting place for newcomers, many of whom were domestic workers who were scattered all over the city. They were social isolates and could only make face-to-face contact with others of like kind on their periodic days off. Apparently Ricketts had also used the Home Service Association (HSA) as his headquarters and had taught many of his music students at this location.

First Meeting Place

Edward (Ed) Smith and his wife Eva, who later became a stalwart at the Jamaican-Canadian Association, lived upstairs the HSA building. Ed was on the board and also functioned as building manager and caretaker. Through their auspices we were able to hold our first and subsequent meetings at this location in the late spring and early summer of 1962. Several persons attended these meetings, among whom were: E. S. Ricketts, George King, Bromley Armstrong, Mel Thompson, Agatha King, Violet King, Ed Smith, Eva Smith, Amy Nelson, Mrs. Holloway, Mrs. Catherine Williams, Roy Williams and Phyllis Whyte. The assembled individuals emerged as an Ad Hoc Group with the sole purpose of planning a Jamaica Independence Celebration.

Independence Celebration Committee

The Ad Hoc Group appointed an Independence Day Celebrations Committee consisting of: Roy Williams, Chairman; Bromley Armstrong, vice-chairman; E. S. Ricketts, secretary; Phyllis Whyte, treasurer; Mrs. Catherine Williams, George King, Leyton Ellis and Kenneth Simpson. This committee was charged with the responsibility of planning and executing the Jamaica Independence Day Celebrations. None of us had any previous experience at this kind of thing. For some reason they chose me to be the chairman.

The committee now embarked energetically on a series of weekly meetings which were rotated from house to house—sometimes at George King's house at 1072 College Street, sometimes at Amy Nelson's apartment on Dupont Street, and sometimes at my house in Scarborough. My recollection is that we appointed subcommittees to tackle some parts of the planning. Bromley Armstrong, vice-chairman of the committee, played a key role in making the arrangements for the celebration. Because he had been around longer than the rest of us, he had many more contacts than the rest of us. He also had many family members who could contribute, and some were later recruited into the Association. We relied on his experience and contacts to help us to make the event a success. He made very worthwhile contributions. In his book it would appear that this event was arranged entirely by him. I need to emphasize that each member of the committee played important roles in bringing it off.

The King Edward Sheraton Hotel

We booked the King Edward Sheraton Hotel on King Street East for our catered banquet. (This was the first barrier that we broke because prior to this, Toronto hotels did not cater or rent to black people.) We communicated with and invited participation from the Federal, Provincial and Municipal governments. They responded and their representatives honoured us by attending and representing their respective levels of government. We had to get copies of the words and music of the new

National Anthem and to listen and to learn the music for the first time. We contacted the Jamaica Government through its new office that was being established in Ottawa. They sent us a tape of the music on reel. However, no one had a reel tape player on which to play it. (By then we had cassette tape recorders.) We improvised. We had to obtain the new flag. I cannot remember where we got it. They also sent us other mementos such as the Coat of Arms, the Motto, the National Bird and the National Flower. We had no financial support. We had to ensure that we sold enough tickets to defray all our expenses, especially that of the King Edward Sheraton Hotel. Our small group worked hard and sold out the function. (Bromley's book indicates that we got financial assistance from the Steelworkers and the United Auto Workers Union. I do not recall that but I cannot refute it.)[5]

The Big Day Arrives

On August 6, 1962 over 250 Jamaicans and their West Indian and Canadian friends dressed in their "Sunday Best" proudly stepped into the King Edward Sheraton Hotel to enjoy a memorable evening. Grace was said by the Rev. C.L.Young, M Th.

The ensuing feast consisted of the following:

Appetizers:
Fruit Fraiche Cocktail
Petit Pain et Beurre,
    Puree de Pois
Coeurs de Celeri Glacee et Olives

Main Course:
Dinde Roti d'Ontario avec Sauce Canneberge
Pomme de Terre Roti, Chaufleur Crème

Dessert:
Tarte Pomme a la Mode

Beverage:
Café ou the

Following dinner a toast was raised to the Queen. The toast to Jamaican Independence was proposed by David Lewis, QC, M.P. and the response was made by Bradley Phillips, M.A. The toast to Canada was proposed by Mr. Stanley Grizzle and the response was by Hon. Allan Grossman, M.P.P. The final toast was to the Commonwealth and was proposed by Mrs. C. V. Callender, M.A. Dr. Stanley Haidasz, M.P. responded.

The highlight of the evening was the unfurling for the first time of our brand new flag. We were enthralled as the Green, the Black and the Gold unfolded before our eyes. We were so proud. We stood stiffly at attention as we listened to the rendition of our National Anthem for the very first time sung by Miss Daughn King and played by E. S. Ricketts, C.D. The spirit of patriotism and oneness was at its highest. We were united. We were proud. We truly embraced the national motto "OUT OF MANY, ONE PEOPLE."

Patron of the event was His Worship Nathan Phillips, Q.C., Mayor of Toronto. Honorary Chairman was Lieut.-Col. B. J. Legge, E.D., C.D. The Chairman was Roy G. Williams, M.A., MComm. See (Exhibit I above).

The celebrants then danced the night away to the pulsating rythms of Lord Power (Eric Armstrong) and his calypso band. The show consisted of a limbo dance competition and the sensational performance of Eric's daughter, 11-year-old Donna Armstrong, who went under the bar six inches from the floor. This performance was declared a new limbo dancing record for Toronto. This was duly reported by the *Toronto Star,* August 7, 1962.

THE AFTERMATH

Many of the celebration participants left that function feeling that there was no obstacle that they could not overcome, no challenge that they could not conquer and no heights that they could not attain. After all they were no longer colonials. They were now proud citizens of an independent nation. They were now on par with all other people. As they basked in the success of the function and the elation and euphoria which ensued, the group felt that it could not and should not end there. They collectively desired to have a vehicle which would enable the occurrence of such functions in the future and would provide a bonding mechanism for the Jamaican and associated communities. The committee immediately embarked on the planning of a New Year's Eve celebration. The people who attended the Independence Day Celebrations desired the formation of a permanent organization. Therefore the Ad Hoc Group which planned the Jamaica Independence celebrations decided to go ahead to create an organization.

The Constitution Committee

A Constitution Committee consisting of Bromley Armstrong, Miss Mavis Magnus, George King, Miss Amy Nelson, Mrs. Violet Carter and Roy Williams was established. Bromley Armstrong was the chairman and Mavis Magnus was the secretary. The committee was commissioned to develop and present a draft constitution for approval at an Organizational Meeting to be called in the near future. Members met on successive weekends, again at their various residences on a rotational basis. There was much heated debate and many conflicts, due to the differing viewpoints, on the vision, the objectives and the wording of various articles. However, they finally hammered out the first draft constitution. The draft constitution's Preamble listed the nine (9) objectives of the Association as follows:

1—To develop and maintain closer relations between Canadians and Jamaicans.
2—To better acquaint Canadians with Jamaican opinions (social, immigration, political, economical, racial, etc.).
3—To establish closer relations with Jamaicans living in Canada and to mold this group into an effective and influential voice in community affairs.
4—To co-operate with West Indians and other National or Territorial groups in pursuing common aims and objectives.
5—To provide a forum for noteworthy Jamaican speakers in Canada.
6—To establish official contact with the Jamaican High Commissioner in Ottawa.
7—To establish and maintain a scholarship fund to assist Jamaican students in Canada.
8—To give assistance to newcomers wherever possible.
9—To establish a Centre for Social and Cultural activities.

It proposed 12 Articles dealing with such matters as the Name (three options), Categories of Membership, Officers and their Duties, The Executive Committee and other Committees, Election of Officers, Finances and Parliamentary Procedures (See Appendix 3). By the middle of September 1962 the committee had completed its task.

TRANSITION TO PERMANENCE

Roy Williams (1962-1966)

The meeting to transform the movement from an ad hoc entity to an established organization took place on September 23, 1962 at the YMCA, 40 College Street (present site of the Metropolitan Toronto Police headquarters). We had sent out notice of meeting to the many people with whom we had come in contact during the previous weeks. We had a large turnout. The meeting, chaired by Roy G. Williams, voted unanimously to accept the draft constitution. It voted unanimously to establish itself as an Association, governed by the constitution it had just approved. It also voted the following ten persons to constitute its first Executive Committee: Roy G. Williams, Bromley Armstrong, George King, Ira Dundas, Miss Mavis Magnus. J. B. Campbell, Owen Tennyson, Miss Phyllis Whyte, Mrs. Violet Carter and Esmund S. Ricketts. Most of the attendees paid their membership fee of $2.00 prior to the start of the meeting and many others subsequent thereto.

First Officers Elected

Immediately following the Organizational Meeting the newly elected Executive Committee convened to appoint its Officers and Chairpersons of various committees. At the first meeting there was no direct election for specific offices. The Constitution provided for the election of a 10-member Executive Committee who would then elect or appoint the officers. The general membership voted a slate of 10 Executive Members who in turn elected officers from among themselves. They appointed the following: President, Roy G. Williams; Vice President, Bromley Armstrong; Executive Secretary, George King; Treasurer, Ira Dundas; Recording and Correspondence Secretary, Miss Mavis Magnus. These were the first officers of the Jamaican-Canadian Association. (See Appendix 4) Three committee chairpersons were appointed as follows: Bromley Armstrong, Chair of the General Purposes Committee; J. B. Campbell, Chair of the Education and Scholarship Committee and Owen Tennyson, Chair of the Publicity and Social Committee. The Jamaican-Canadian Association (JCA) was born. It was the first such Caribbean national organization and was the model patterned by other Caribbean groups as they too emerged, in rapid succession, from colonial to independent status.

"Founders" and Founding Members

It is important to clarify the issue as to who is a "Founding Member." It would appear to me that all those persons who attended the Organization Meeting on September 23, 1962 and paid their membership, in addition to those who participated in any of the preparatory work done for this event would qualify as a "Founding Member" of the Association. There are therefore 237 "Founding Members."(See Appendix 5) The first Officers and Executive, however, are those named in the above paragraph. If one desires to fine tune the terminology even further to define "Founders" that would be those members who were engaged in the preparatory activities—especially the drafting of the constitution—preparatory to the convening of the Inaugural Organization Meeting. Those persons were Bromley Armstrong, Mavis Magnus, Roy Williams, George King, Amy Nelson and Vi Carter. This is intended to finally clarify the issues of "Founders", "Founding Members" and First Executive Committee.

Not all of the "Founders" were on the "First Executive Committee"—Amy Nelson was not. There were some on the first Executive committee who were not "Founders"—J. B. Campbell, Ira Dundas, Owen Tennyson, and Phyllis Whyte. If one wanted to be all inclusive one could merge both groups. This would then include Amy Nelson but exclude Frank Magnus who was the replacement for J. B. Campbell who did not stand for re-election in March, 1963. The revised "Founders" list would now read alphabetically—Bromley Armstrong, J. B. Campbell, Vi Carter, Ira Dundas, George King, Mavis Magnus, Amy Nelson, Owen Tennyson, E. S. Ricketts. Roy Williams, Phyllis Whyte. The new categorization then is "Founders," "Founding or First Executive" and "Founding Members."

Getting Started

Up to this point we had been meeting in people's homes. Now, however, we needed an official meeting place, an office from which to conduct our business. We needed an address, a telephone, office equipment, a boardroom. We also needed a place where we could meet informally for social gatherings.

The first offer of accommodation was made by Winston McKenzie, who with Dick Smith and others operated Club Tropics, a West Indian weekend night club upstairs 12 Queen Street East in downtown Toronto. We gratefully accepted this offer and held one or two meetings there. While this space served for Executive Committee meetings and even the occasional general meeting it was unsuitable for normal office functions.

Our First Office

Where would we receive responses to the volume of correspondence we were beginning to generate? We needed a postal address. George King, our Executive Secretary came to the rescue on this one. He arranged for us to get a post office box at the main postal station at Front and Bay Streets. Thus for many years as the JCA moved from place to place our post office address remained constant at P.O. Box 532, Terminal "A", Toronto. This address was soon shared with the Jamaican-Canadian (Toronto) Credit Union Limited after it was established in 1963.

Still we needed an office. Our activities were increasing at an enormous rate. Our next benefactor to the rescue was Lloyd C. Perry. Q.C. Lloyd was the Deputy Official Guardian for the Province of Ontario (later promoted to be the Official Guardian). He was a Canadian of Jamaican parentage. His father had been a bishop in one of the black churches. He was interested in aiding groups in the black community. He was proud of his Jamaican heritage and he took a liking to us. He managed to get us some unused space at 85 Lombard Street (near Jarvis St.) This was upstairs the liquor store and across from the morgue (at the time). We had an office but we had no furniture. We got desks, chairs and other odds and sorts either from donations or from stuff we bought at auctions at bargain prices (for which I got my knuckles rapped sometimes). This is reported in Bromley Armstrong's Memoirs[6]. We acquired a typewriter and an old Mimeograph machine which we used to pump out the early newsletters. The space was not plush but it provided a base from which to operate. Best of all it was FREE (or the rent was minimal). This space served us very well for a while—a year or two, I guess, but then came the word that the landlord (whom we never knew) wanted the space back. We had to give it up. This was the end of our first JCA office—85 Lombard Street, Toronto.

Fortunately, our benefactor had powerful connections and he soon found us another space at 29 Colborne Street, just south of King Street near to Church Street and right behind the King Edward Sheraton Hotel.

We moved our stuff over to the new location and we were still in business. Our postal address remained constant. Lloyd Perry, Q.C. became our first Honorary Member and this was well deserved.

In those early days each of us worked like beavers. Our Executive Committee was strong, enthusiastic, cohesive and highly motivated as we took on our various assignments to build the organization and serve our members. I remember working long hours and late into many nights with our Recording Secretary, Mavis Magnus. She was a secretary and worked at the Canadian Broadcasting Corporation (CBC) at their former Jarvis Street location. She was super efficient, very professional and a hard worker. We would have office hours for the association in the late afternoons and on weekends. Mavis would walk down from her Jarvis Street office to our JCA office on Lombard Street or Colborne Street. I would walk down from my office at Ryerson Institute (at the time) now Ryerson University and we would start to work. We would deal with telephone calls and incoming correspondence which was picked up and delivered by George King and we would generate the outgoing communication. Our outgoing correspondence was always professionally done because Mavis was a professional and she set a high standard for the image of the JCA as reflected in its correspondence. In addition we mailed out notice of meetings and our quarterly newsletters which we cranked out on the aforementioned Mimeograph machine, which might have been the last one in existence and which I picked up at an auction of office equipment.

I would get scolded, mostly by Bromley, for acquiring needed, used office equipment which was obtained at bargain prices. We could not operate the office efficiently without equipment and I would obtain what I thought was needed as they became available, usually in the interval between monthly Executive Committee meetings. I would pay with my own money with the expectation of being reimbursed. The argument then developed around reimbursement for the money spent in that it was not previously authorized by the Executive. The Executive Committee then parsimoniously placed a ceiling of $50.00 on the amount that the president could spend without prior Executive Committee approval. Clearly nothing of any consequence could be bought for under $50.00.[7] However, by then we had already acquired what was needed to run the office. The old Mimeograph machine did a wonderful job in enabling us to keep the communication going with our members well beyond the expiration of my term of office. I do not regret any of the expenditures. They were all very necessary. Not only was I the president, I was also the association's chief operating officer and we could not operate in an empty space. We were a "Start Up" operation, building from the bottom up.

The mindset reflected in the above incident pervaded many of the early decisions of the JCA Executive and highlighted some ideological differences. Some vocal board members were fiscal conservatives, some had socio-political-economic orientations that made them very wary and timid about investments and expenditures. Others were more entrepreneurial and inclined toward future potential and investments. With this mindset we shied away from even attempting to acquire the old Mount Sinai Nurses Residence on Yorkville Avenue which was then available for sale at the then paltry sum of $15,000.00 which today is worth Hundreds of Thousands of Dollars (even millions). This ideological difference would in later years lead to the first schism within the Association where some members hived off to behave in more entrepreneurial ways.

In those early days we had a lot of fun while at the same time we worked very hard to establish the Association. We had informal gatherings, house parties and periodic dances to generate funds for the association as the small membership fee ($2.00) could not finance the association. The Social Committee chaired by Owen Tennyson was active. In addition to the dances we had theatre nights in Toronto as well as in Stratford, trips to the 1000 Islands and Niagara Falls, Picnics and Fun Days and Bun and Cheese parties at Easter time. On more than one occasion there was a Charter flight to Jamaica at Christmastime. We celebrated our National Independence Days and we had fun at our New Year's Eve parties. These activities aided in group bonding and enhanced cohesiveness. Members had plenty of occasions and opportunity to get to know each other and befriend each other. We were "youngish" to "middle-ageish." (Jamaicanese expressions).

We had membership campaigns with prizes presented to the person who signed up the largest number of new members. I remember Esmund S. Ricketts as the first person to win the first prize for bringing in the most new members. We were proud of our association and we were not reluctant to invite others to join us and in those days the composition of the membership was truly Jamaican and Canadian with a sprinkling of other Caribbean nationals. The JCA became a meeting place and a home away from home for newly arriving immigrants who were coming not only directly from the West Indies but also from the United Kingdom as thousands of West Indians were re-migrating to Canada. It was an important place and a safe place for the predominantly female immigrants (nurses, teachers and household workers) to meet other female and male companions.

Early Jamaica Government Connections

Item number 6 on our list of objectives states "To establish official contact with the Jamaican High Commission in Ottawa". We took this matter very seriously. Right from the outset we contacted the High Commissioner and invited him to visit with us in Toronto. The heaviest concentration of Jamaicans in Canada was and continues to be in the Greater Toronto area. The Jamaican Government needed to be aware of this and to be prepared to service this population. Our February, 1963 Newsletter contained this notice. "A Meeting, Date: Monday, February, 18, 1963. Place: Trinity College Buttery, University of Toronto. Time 7:30 p.m. Reason: To hear Jamaica's Ambassador to Canada, His Excellency E. A. Maynier, O.B.E., on the occasion of his first visit to Toronto." An impressive number of Jamaicans attended to welcome and interact with the High Commissioner.

Intercession for Consulate in Toronto

This was the start of a long and cordial relationship with the High Commission. Each successive High Commissioner has made Toronto a must visit quite early in his/her tenure. Very early in the game we interceded with the Jamaican government to establish an office in Toronto to deal with Jamaican citizens. It was too inconvenient to have to do business long distance through Ottawa. The only Jamaican official in Toronto was Mr. Danny Powell, The Trade Commissioner. It was not until 1970 that a Jamaica Government Regional Information Office was established in Toronto with Mr. Oswald (Ossie) Murray as the Regional Information officer. In 1973 we again made representation to the Jamaican government to establish at least a Passport Office in Toronto. We continued to badger the government until a full consular office was established in 1977 with Len Coke as Consul and with Mr. "Ossie" Murray as the first full-fledged Consul General to Toronto. He was an excellent Consul General. He empathized with the Jamaican people and had a good working relationship with the JCA. He was followed by the late Kay Baxter, the late Marguerite St. Juste and a succession of other excellent Consuls and Consuls General Mr. Herman Lamont, Mr. A.B. Stewart Stephenson, Ms Vivia Betton, Ms Ann-Marie Bonner to the present Consul-General to Toronto, Mr. Seth George Ramocan.

JCA and Activism

While we provided a vehicle for social interaction and national patriotism we also had another major function and role that was not envisioned when the Association was formed. That was to be a voice for the voiceless, to champion causes for the disadvantaged, to represent the unrepresented and to be a bastion against inequity, racism and discrimination. We had hardly become established when we were presented with our first case. It must have been late 1962 or in January of 1963 because I included a report on the incident in our February, 1963 newsletter. As it is now so it was then. It was a complaint against the Toronto police. This young lady worked downtown at the Canadian Broadcasting Company (CBC) on the late afternoon shift. Her home was on Drewry Avenue in North York (north of Finch Avenue). In those days this would be way, way up town. She had finished her shift and was on her way home at night. She was roughly accosted by a police officer who questioned her right to be in that part of town at that time of the night. Her protestations and supplied information that she was on her way to her home was of no avail. He did not believe that a black person could live in that section of Toronto (actually North York). She was detained and further interrogated. She was frightened, intimidated, embarrassed and offended. We took the case. We contacted the Toronto police chief and protested the action of the officer. We requested an investigation of the situation and an apology to the lady as she was not violating any law and the police had no reason to suspect that she was about to commit a crime. In due time, we got the apology from the chief. The chief and another officer actually came to my house in Scarborough to discuss the matter and deliver the apology. This was the first victory that confirmed our authenticity and established that we did need an organization that could intervene on the behalf of others in the community.

The General Purposes Committee, chaired by Vice-President Bromley Armstrong, was the Advocacy, Intervention and Representational arm of the Association, Bromley, due to his prior involvement with other organizations and with the labour movement was ideally suited to this task. He could smell injustice and discrimination from a mile away and he would zero in on it like a beacon. He was kept very busy. Immigration was foremost among the many issues of concern to the Caribbean community. Canada at that time still had a pro-white and anti-black immigration policy. Black applicants for entrance into Canada had immense obstacles to overcome which generally resulted in rejection. The few that made it as far as the then

Toronto International Airport were sometimes "captured" and detained pending deportation often without the opportunity to communicate with anyone to seek help or even for some to contact their relatives. Those who managed to get in on a temporary basis—either as a student, visitor or short-term labor—had a very difficult time to change their status and often required the intervention of the JCA or other high profile community advocates such as Harry Gairey Sr. of the West Indies Federation Club (WIF) or earlier Don Moore of the then Negro Citizenship Association.

First brief on Immigration

It was no surprise then that the first major action of the General Purposes Committee was to convene a "Conference on West Indian Immigration to Canada." This was convened on October 5, 1963 at the Steelworkers Centre, 33 Cecil Street, Toronto. In the morning session top ranking panelists Andrew Brewin, Q.C., M.P., Douglas Morton, Q.C., and Dr. Stanley Haidasz, M.P. spoke to the shortcomings and discriminatory nature of the Immigration Act and the urgent need for reform. In the afternoon session Bradley Phillips spoke on "The Goals and Accomplishments of West Indians in Canada." Following a spirited discussion the conference concluded with the attendees appending their signatures to the Brief that had been prepared to be presented to the Minister of Immigration in Ottawa. This Brief was duly presented and we continued over the years to have a dialogue with the government on immigration matters and the conversion to a non-discriminatory immigration policy and practice. Immigration was one of the most thorny issues in those early days. This complex immigration situation led to the emergence of an immigration consulting industry with some among them being charlatans who sometimes bilked their defenseless clients.

Other Thorny Issues

In addition to immigration the other issues of prime concern were employment, housing, policing, and education, among others. Prejudice and discrimination showed its face in so many ways and in so many different places. In employment the reasons for rejection were not only you are "not qualified", but you are "too qualified" or you have "no Canadian experience" unless you were applying for a janitor's job or some other low-paying unskilled service jobs. Black males were primarily employed as porters on the trains operated by the Canadian National and the Canadian Pacific

Railways. For the black teenagers it practically made no sense to finish high school or go on to university as the prospect of employment at the end of the road was almost nil, except for the railroads or janitorial jobs.

In housing the response to an attempt to rent a room or apartment was "Sorry it's already rented." The "For Rent" sign would still be in the window a week or two later or the advertisement would still be running in the newspaper for the same address. There were some who were so blatant as to post a notice on the front door or window—"No Blacks." Some slammed the door in your face.

In policing it was not uncommon for black men to be frequently stopped and questioned by police under the guise of having a strong resemblance to someone on their wanted list. If you were driving a motor car the likelihood of being stopped and questioned was very high and the more expensive or new your vehicle was the greater the likelihood that you would be stopped and questioned for no apparent reason other than you are black. It was not uncommon also for the information broadcast over the radio about someone the police was seeking to apprehend, that that someone spoke with a "Jamaican accent."

Hotels, restaurants and bars were not welcoming to black people. Some would refuse to serve you and they would let you know that you were not welcome in their establishment. These battles remained to be fought. These are documented in Bromley Armstrong's memoirs.

In education the school systems failed to properly adapt to the changing school population and responded by "streaming" the black children into lower-achieving and non-academic programs which would predestine them to a life of servility. This too needed to be challenged.

Ontario Human Rights

The Ontario Human Rights Commission (OHRC) was established in 1961 to administer the Ontario Human Rights Code which was the codification of all of the anti-discriminatory legislation previously passed by the Ontario Government. The *Toronto Star* October 10, 1963 reported "112 allegations of discrimination were dealt with by the Ontario Human Rights Commission last year, said Commission Director, Dr. Daniel Hill. All were settled out of court by conciliation. Most of the complaints were from Negroes refused housing or accommodation because of their colour".

An early report of the General Purposes Committee, September 8, 1963 reads as follows: "Your committee is very pleased to report we have had final settlements on three cases referred to the Ontario Human Rights

Commission covering discrimination in employment, housing and public accommodation. Letters of apologies were sent to complainants in all cases assuring them of compliance with the Human Rights Code of the Province, and assuring them of no restrictive policies towards any group or individual. Following the press release by the Commission letters were also sent to our organization (the JCA) thanking us for the assistance we gave on these cases and our efforts in bringing this to the attention of the Commission. We were able to find accommodation for newcomers and others looking for flats, boarding and apartments. Demands for accommodation are on the increase and we require information on places available."[8]

In addition to the above our input and involvement was beginning to be sought on a wide range of issues. We met with the Social Planning Council of Metropolitan Toronto, Immigration Branch as well as the Family and Child Branch and participated in their discussions about immigration and the issues surrounding the assimilation of non-white immigrants and also the adoption of non-white children.

In the years 1962 through to 1966, JCA was very busy dealing with the multiplicity of issues as detailed in the above samples. The society was changing very fast. New immigrants of a darker hue were beginning to stream into the country in increasing numbers as the Immigration Act changed and the host country did not quite know how to accommodate and instantly adapt to this new reality. The old institutions, culture, norms and values were deeply entrenched and were strongly resistant to change. The newly arrived immigrants expected to be respected and to be treated fairly. They were not inclined to accept discrimination, inferiority and inequity in so many aspects of their everyday lives. The stage was clearly set for conflict as new standards and protocols needed to be discovered, developed and negotiated at all levels of government and the society. The JCA had an important role to play.

Legal Structure

During this period we had been careful to place the Association on a sound legal footing. We had drafted the constitution and we requested A. C. McRobie, QC, a Bay Street lawyer who had previously done some work for Roy Williams, to get the association incorporated. At the time we visualized the JCA to be a national organization with chapters across Canada, similar to the concept later developed by the National Association of Jamaicans and Supportive Organizations in Canada. As a consequence we instructed our lawyer to obtain a Federal incorporation so we could operate nationally.

We had big dreams even then. McRobie got the Association incorporated but there followed an argument within the Executive Committee as to whether he would keep the charter in his office or the JCA should have physical possession of the charter. Lawyers traditionally keep the charters of companies on behalf of their clients. There was also some argument about the paltry fee of about $150.00 plus disbursements. Some members of the Executive felt that since we paid for it we should have it and keep it. We were not sophisticated enough for a lawyer of McRobie's stature and the relationship soon ended. I think the charter became a victim of the Dawes Road fire some years later, which would not have been the case had we heeded the lawyer's advice and allowed him to safeguard the charter. I believe the JCA subsequently obtained provincial incorporation in Ontario.

Creation of a Credit Union

Another thing we did was to create the Jamaican-Canadian (Toronto) Credit Union Ltd. We wanted our newly arriving immigrants as well as those who were already established to have a vehicle through which they could save and borrow based on their collective savings. We were strong believers in the Co-Operative movement and we believed that we could collectively build an economic base that would be beneficial to the community. Members could conduct their saving and borrowing transactions in privacy within a comfortable, non-bureaucratic environment and with people of their own kind. In addition members had the responsibility to manage their own financial institution and to serve on its various committees. The credit union functioned for many years—well into the 1990's—when it was persuaded to bite off more than it could chew by moving to a high cost rental site and had to be dissolved. A very sad day for the community. **This is more fully discussed in a later section**

Term of Office Ends

When we designed the constitution our intention was that this organization would function on democratic principles. We wanted the voice and wishes of the people to be paramount. Decisions would be made by majority vote whether in general meetings or in the various committees. We did not intend for anyone to monopolize any position or to function in a dictatorial manner. Therefore when my term of office expired in March, 1966 it was time to step down, which I did. I had served almost four years as president.

As in any organization conflicts and disagreements do occur. Within the Executive Committee there had developed an ideological divide. There were some of us who advocated that a parallel economic entity be established where we could pool our resources to make investments, acquire real estate and take advantage of opportunities which presented themselves so that we would have some economic clout in the society. In addition we felt that there was a need for a building to conduct social activities where people could meet and enjoy themselves in a relaxed, comfortable, non-discriminatory and non-threatening environment. There was a crying need for a social meeting place. This concept was anathema to those on the Executive who were of a different socio-economic-political persuasion and those fiscal conservatives who felt that we should not dabble in any business ventures. The level of risk averseness was very high and their spokespersons were very persuasive. That group carried the day. It was time for me to leave.

John Brooks, Amy Nelson, Frank Wallace, J. B. Campbell and Roy Williams then formed and operated the Latin Quarter Club at 290½ Yonge Street (partial site of the present Eaton Centre) from the late 1960's to well into the late 1970's. It was the hot spot for Friday and Saturday night entertainment for all those years and many a lifelong connection was made there. It was the place where the newly arriving Caribbean immigrants met and associated with each other. Expropriation for development of the Eaton Centre ended that venture. Many JCA meetings were held at that location before it was able to acquire its own premises. The only other social meeting space for West Indians was the West Indies Federation Club (WIF Club) located on Brunswick Avenue at College Street. (This building was later destroyed by fire)

Last Half of the Decade (1966-1971)

Mel Thompson (1966-1971)

During the years 1967 to 1980 Roy was not involved with the JCA and did not have first-hand knowledge of the internal workings of the Association. What is known is that Mel Thompson was elected and became the second president. He was a "Founding Member" of the JCA since its inception, another university graduate. I do not know his resume in 1962 but Mel later became a professor of economics at Ryerson University and, while not in the same department, he was a colleague of mine at that institution until we both retired. The task before him would have been enormous. He would have had to continue to strengthen the foundations of the young association and to pilot it through its growth and stabilize it in a highly turbulent environment. He would be destined to serve in that capacity on more than one occasion. His first term lasted from early 1966 through to early 1971.

There was some anti discrimination legislation on the books, e.g. Fair Accommodations Practices Act, Fair Employment Practices Act and the Ontario Human Rights Commission which administered the Ontario Human Rights Code. The society had not changed substantially from what it was in the 1950's to the late 1960's and 1970's. Discrimination, racial prejudice and unfair treatment still abounded in housing, in employment, in the school system, in police-community relations, in social justice and employment fairness issues. There was a huge battle still to be fought for civil and human rights for Jamaican, West Indian and other non-white immigrants.

At the federal level the immigration gate had become slightly ajar with the passage of a new Immigration Act in 1952. It, however, was still strongly biased against non-white but highly favourable to white immigrants. Being a British subject or the citizen of another Commonwealth country was of no benefit or advantage, despite the frantic and sustained efforts by various organizations and individuals to persuade successive governments to remove the barriers.

The pressures for West Indians to emigrate during this period were very powerful as the doors to the United States and The United Kingdom were closing. Canada became the next relief outlet. West Indian migration to Canada between 1960-1969 totalled 46,030. This represented 3.34 per cent of total Canadian immigration for that period. This figure more than tripled in the following decade 1970-1979 when 159,216 now representing 11.02 per cent of Canadian immigration, entered the country."[9]

"Between 1965 and 1979 a total of 193,480 Caribbean immigrants entered Canada, just under 40 per cent of these were from Jamaica. Approximately 67 per cent of these settled in Ontario and the majority of these settled in the Greater Toronto Area."[10]

A cursory examination of these statistics brings into focus the tremendous demands that were placed on the JCA to respond to the calls for service from a rapidly increasing immigrant population. The calls for intervention at the immigration office and at the ports of entry escalated exponentially. Demand for assistance in the assimilation and adaptation process was extremely high. There was a need to respond to the increasing need for affordable housing. The increasing number of black people on the streets generated an increasing number of encounters with the police. Many reported being stopped and questioned for no good reason, and thus the start of a trend. More black people being arrested. More black people being convicted and the increase in the numbers of black males in the jails. The criminalization of the black male population had begun.

There were appeals against unfair treatment when people applied for jobs for which they were eminently qualified and were rejected on the pretext of "no Canadian experience," or for being "too qualified." They needed to be represented at the Human Rights Commission to have their cases adjudicated. Then there were the children in the school system who were being wasted by being "streamed" into low-level, dead-end classes and programs leading to no prospect of engaging in higher education or professional qualification. All of the above required a high level of activisim and visibility. The JCA had unwittingly come into existence at a most opportune time. There was no other organization from the black/Caribbean Community that was properly organized and sufficiently stable to respond to these enormous challenges.

All of these responses were being made by volunteers. There was no paid staff. Mel Thompson and his board and committees rendered yeoman service to the community and kept the Association alive and kicking. There was no government subsidy. The Association was self funded. It had to hold dances, raffles and other fund-raising activities to stay alive. And in those days the membership fee was a paltry $2.00 per year. There is not enough kudos that can be handed out to Mel Thompson and his various committees for the services rendered. That ended the decade of the 1960's, as Mel relinquished the presidency in February, 1971.

Recollections by Former President Mel Thompson

What started as a social organization soon developed as the community organization with diverse demands from the general Jamaican community to address or mediate problems encountered by the black Community. It was apparent that most of these problems were not adjustment problems but were due to matters of race and colour.

The Ontario Human Rights Commission

Fortunately the Ontario Government responded with sympathy to the numerous complaints by Jamaicans and other non white immigrants. The

Ontario Government, sensitive to numerous complaints by immigrants, had established the Ontario Human Rights Commission in 1961 and the newly appointed Director, Dr. Daniel G. Hill, was quite aggressive in reported cases of discrimination not only in work but in everything. The Association pursued a number of cases where there was perceived to be violation of the Ontario Human Rights Code; a notable example was the case of discrimination against a United States steel company which had refused to employ some black welders. The company was fined and was made to pay large amounts to the five welders who were directly affected. There were numerous other cases in which the Association was involved and demanded and obtained concessions.

Housing Discrimination

Altogether the Jamaican-Canadian Association (JCA) aggressively pursued the enforcement of human rights in Employment and Housing in the case of discrimination in housing we organized a team of white volunteers to test the system. Our approach generally was partially responsible for the virtual end of racial discrimination in employment and housing in this province.

The Henningham Case

The celebrated Henningham case (a domestic worker) brought the Association a lot of exposure and unjustified criticism. Vinette Henningham worked with a wealthy family in a well-to-do neighbourhood, and accidentally drowned in the family's swimming pool. Unknown to the JCA she was buried as an unknown pauper. The *Toronto Star* got wind of it and did not hesitate to blame the JCA about this tragic incident of this woman being buried in a pauper's plot. This incident generated a lot of public interest and the *Star* opened a fund (The Henningham Fund) and the public responded generously. The JCA paid for the transportation and burial for Vinette in Jamaica. An Executive of the Association accompanied the body to the hills of Clarendon for the funeral; the *Toronto Star* report was very vivid; you could hear the people singing "Home Once More" a local Jamaica favourite. The surplus from the fund was placed in trust and later sent to the Jamaica Government.

The Albert Johnson Case

Another tragedy: The Albert Johnson Case. A police officer shot and killed Albert Johnson, an unarmed man descending the stairs of his house off Vaughn Road. His wife called the President of the JCA and requested help. We organized a large Memorial Service. Tempers of the community were ignited. The President gave the address.

From its early years the JCA developed early learning Saturday morning programs with projects in the Jane-Finch area and one at Lawrence Heights. Recreation basketball and some high school academics were blended in the program. Youth benefited from the programs.

Certification of Jamaican Teachers

After years and numerous complaints about the refusal to accept certification of graduates from Jamaica's Teacher Training Colleges the Ontario Minister of Education, on frequent complaints by the JCA, finally permitted them.

Immigration Resolutions

General Immigration of Jamaicans and persons overstaying their visa was a matter of great concern causing frequent appeals to the Canadian Minister of Immigration in Ottawa. Finally, he decided that the local officer in charge should meet with the President of the JCA and try to resolve the problems and avoid frequent submissions to him.

Part 2

The Decade of the 1970's (1971-1980)

Bromley Armstrong (1971-1972)

It would take five (5) different presidents to take the JCA through this decade. Mel Thompson demitted office in early 1971 and Bromley Armstrong was elected to become the JCA's third president. Bromley was with the association before it was founded and therefore is a genuine "Founder." He was the chairman of the committee that drafted the first constitution and he was elected to the first Executive Committee and became the first Vice President and chairman of the General Purposes Committee. He had an extensive resume as a champion for the disadvantaged, underprivileged, underrepresented and as a lifelong civil and human rights advocate. This has been detailed elsewhere in this document and in his own Memoirs[11]. He was part of the organizing committee for the commemoration of Jamaica's Independence in 1962. He had the credentials and background to become an able president of the JCA. He had impressive contacts with movers and shakers within the Labour Union Movement, within the CCF (which later became the New Democratic Party), and with various human and civil rights advocates.

Bromley was always a powerful voice for the JCA and the black community. All the conditions detailed above that prevailed during Mel Thompson's term in office would obtain during Bromley's term, as the immigration flood gates literally burst open and thousands of entrants from the Caribbean and elsewhere needed to be attended to. This involved dealing individually with hundreds of immigrants with problems as well as dealing with the governmental and non-governmental establishments that were causing them grief. It was a gargantuan task but it was one that he had been involved with even before the association was founded, as he previously had been heavily involved with other organizations, including the Negro Citizenship Association.

The Association, still headquartered in two rooms at 29 Colborne Street, found it quite difficult and inconvenient when it needed to assemble for quarterly and Annual General Meetings and when it needed a place to conduct the regular socials, get-togethers and dances. It had to hold meetings at the YMCA, YMHA, Ontario Credit Union Building, Ontario Federation of Labour Building, OISE, The Steelworkers Union Hall and elsewhere. Fundraising dances were held in rented halls, e.g. Royal Canadian Legion Halls, Columbus Hall, Ukrainian Hall, church halls and others. The JCA geographically had to rotate these events east, west, north and south to facilitate the members who had begun to be dispersed throughout the Greater Toronto Area (GTA). The JCA was literally a peripatetic organization wandering from place to place in the city. We even began to envy the other communities who had their own places.

JCA Acquires its First Home

It was always an objective of the JCA, as stated in its Constitution, to have a home of its own. Objective Number Nine states "To establish a centre for social and cultural activities." (Appendix 3) The officers were, therefore, continuously on the lookout for a suitable building in a desirable location.

In February 1971, after scouring the city for a number of months, Canute Cato, the Executive Secretary, of the JCA happened upon a For Sale sign at 65 Dawes Road, the East Toronto Veterans' Memorial Hall. He quickly alerted Bromley to his find and they proceeded to examine the property. They were excited about this and not wanting to lose out on it they promptly made an offer to purchase the property for $57,500. Bromley made the down payment of $7,000.00 out of his own pocket and together with Cato gave two post dated cheques and two (2) mortgages to seal the deal. There was a first mortgage of $25,000 at 10% interest to mature in five years and a second mortgage of $20,000 at 10% interest to mature in 10 years. The deal was done. This was bold and decisive action. Missing was the temporizing and the extensive deliberation and debates as to the wisdom of taking action and whether they would be able to pay for it. The naysayers were denied the opportunity to naysay. Even more startling was the fact that the deal closed at the end of March, 1971. These two officers had been in their respective offices a mere four weeks following their election in February.

Jamaica House

65 Dawes Road, Toronto

There was elation and jubilation in the entire Caribbean community, but Jamaicans were especially proud. Finally they had acquired a place of their own. A meeting place. A place to hang out; a place to play domino; a place to hold meetings; a place to have parties and a headquarters and offices for the JCA. No more need for peripatetic wanderings all over the city. The entire Caribbean community's interest in the JCA skyrocketed because now there was something tangible to which they could relate. Membership in the Association went through the roof although the Membership dues had recently been increased by 50 per cent to $3.00 per year. They now wanted to be a part of something that was alive and kicking. It was their organization and it gave them voice.

But there was work to be done; 65 Dawes Road in East End Toronto, was an old building. It needed renovations and modifications. The call went out for workers from the community to bring their tools, their skills and their labour. They came in droves—men, women and children. It was their Association, their building. It was like a miniature Habitat for Humanity.

Grand Opening

His Excellency, Mr. V. C. Smith, High Commissioner of Jamaica to Canada, welcoming the Guest and saying a word of Commendation at the opening of Jamaica House.

Once all the repairs and modifications were completed there was a grand opening of the building in May, 1971. His Excellency V. C. Smith, the High Commissioner for Jamaica came from Ottawa to cut the ribbon to open the building. Mr. Oswald Murray, the new Regional Information Officer in Toronto (there was no Consulate as yet); Mr. Danny Powell, the Jamaica Trade Commissioner; and local politicians and dignitaries participated. The building was officially named JAMAICA HOUSE. A grand celebration ensued. Many moments of joy was experienced by the attendants. For the remainder of 1971 and into the first few months of 1972 the place hummed with activity. These included conferences, workshops, seminars, women's craft and sewing groups and domino and social evenings on the weekends. They even hosted a group from the United States.

Black Saturday

Unfortunately and sadly the joy, euphoria and satisfaction was short lived as in May, 1972, a fire of unknown origin mysteriously and totally destroyed JAMAICA HOUSE. There were suspicions that the fire was deliberately set by those who hated our kind. But nothing was proven. The hopes of the community were dashed as it had lost not only the building but all its contents—furniture, fixtures, equipment, utensils, and worst of all irreplaceable records of the previous 10 years. Lost too was Bromley's down payment on the building. It was disastrous. The community was devastated.

The Association reverted to its peripatetic ways by first obtaining temporary shelter at Bromley's office at 200 O'Connor Drive. It then moved to 984 Pape Avenue, then 253 Danforth Road as it started the long, excruciating and frustrating search for another permanent home. Bromley, who was self employed, relinquished the presidency in 1972 having served just one year. His legacy was the acquisition of the JAMAICA HOUSE.

Mel Thompson Returns to Office (1972-1975)

Bromley demitted office in 1972 and faithful trooper, Mel Thompson, was brought back into harness as president to pilot the JCA through the next few very difficult years until 1975 when he took another break from office. All of the issues that previously existed continued to exist but in greater numbers and wider variety. Police-community relations remained intractable. Education issues multiplied throughout the city and its various boroughs as the increasing number of children continued to be misunderstood and consequently inappropriately treated. Innovative methods had to be developed. Consultative committees had to be designed and populated, all with volunteer bodies. Employment discrimination continued and representation needed to be made to the Ontario Human Rights Commission on behalf of those who were unfairly treated. Immigration problems continued.

There were briefs to be prepared and submitted and representations to be made at each and every level of government. Members were beginning to be scattered all across the GTA. There was a constant stream of calls for various services and so few bodies with available spare time to respond.

There was money to be raised to pay the association's bills and there was a building to be found for a permanent home and money to be found to fund it. It was not a simple task but Mel Thompson stayed aboard and kept the ship afloat. The Association can never ever repay Mel for holding the fort through those lean, hard years; and when he was not president, he held other offices. He seemed to be on every Executive Committee from 1966 through to 1981. He again served the association as First Vice-President in 1992. He then retired after valiantly serving his people for more than 30 years. Mel Thompson more than did his part.

10th Anniversary Celebrations

During this period two landmark events took place. The first was in 1972 when the Association celebrated its 10th anniversary. This was a gala affair which was celebrated at Columbus Hall. This first decennial anniversary was a significant milestone because the association had survived from its infancy and had overcome enormous obstacles, both internally and externally. Traditionally, organizations with a predominantly black membership tended not to survive for ten years. This was significant. The accompanying photographs show the small group cutting the 10th Anniversary cake as they posed for celebratory photographs.

Prime Minister Pays a Visit

Prime Minister of Jamaica
Commonwealth Conference, Ottawa, August 1973

The other significant event occurred in 1973 the Association's 11th year. It had the high honour of having Prime Minister the Hon. Michael Manley and Mrs. Manley as its guests at the 11th Anniversary and Independence Celebration held at the Royal York Hotel on August 11, 1973. President Mel Thompson stated "We are more than elated that 'our' Prime Minister, the Hon. Michael Manley and Mrs. Manley are our special guests this evening. We welcome them and their party. We commend him and his government also for the new initiatives taken to build a new Jamaica economically and attitudinally, and pray that the mind and eyes of all Jamaica may be opened."[12] Ron King, the Social Committee Chairman, notes in the September, 1973 issue of the JCA Newsletter, "Our 11th Independence Dance on August 11th is an affair that is being talked about and will be talked about for a long time. The band was superb and those who attended enjoyed themselves until the last note was sounded. Prime Minister Manley stayed with us until the very end. It was obvious he was pleased. Toronto did enjoy our Prime Minister too—he was truly an Ambassador."[13]

The Latter Half of the 1970's (1975-1980)

From 1962 through to 1975 there had only been three presidents of the JCA but the period from 1975 through to 1980 there were five (5) presidents if we include Mel Thompson who served twice during this period. The length of their terms in office varied from a low of six months to a high of two years with two presidents, each serving one-year terms. This high turnover of presidents during this time is reflective of the arduous nature of the task during that turbulent period which required copious amounts of volunteer time in a highly volatile situation. All, with the exception of Canute Cato were full time educators who had to try to fit the JCA in with their full time academic responsibilities. It was not an easy task. One still wonders how Mel Thompson did it.

Canute J. Cato (1975-1977)

The immediate successor to Mel Thompson was Canute J. Cato who took over the presidency in 1975 and served until 1977 (the longest spell). In his day job he was an accomplished accountant and auditor. He had been on the Executive Committee as early as 1967 and had served two (2) terms as the Executive Secretary. He was very involved, together with Bromley, in the purchase of "JAMAICA HOUSE" in 1971 and was devastated when it burned to the ground in 1972. He, therefore, was highly motivated and committed to the reacquisition of a replacement Jamaica House. Cato's energy and time in office was devoted almost exclusively to achieving this goal. He had set a target for the acquisition and completion of the Community Centre Project by 1976. Unfortunately some mistakes were made with the disposition of the land at 65 Dawes Road. As a consequence the land was sold for a lesser amount than could have been obtained from a previous offer. That money was placed into a special Building Fund account toward the acquisition of the next building. There ensued a continuing search for suitable replacement sites.

New Site Acquired

An unused former TTC site at 3391-3393 Danforth Avenue was identified and the land was purchased for $115,000 in 1975. The Association began to negotiate with the City of Scarborough regarding zoning, building plans and permits, with architects and designers and finally with funders, externally and internally. Unfortunately there was an error in costing the project. The actual cost would be quite a bit higher than originally calculated. In addition there was a new Scarborough Building Code By-Law of which the group was unaware. Complying with this would have increased the cost even further. In the final analysis everything came apart due to the inability to finalize the funding component. An application to Wintario for funds was not successful. Wintario had approved $138,000 if the JCA could match it. This proved to be the sticking point. Other government funding was not forthcoming; and as was the case with the first building, those who were willing to promise were not as willing to sign on the dotted line when the chips were down. They were not as willing to back up words with action.

An Unpleasant Conclusion

The JCA held the land on Danforth Avenue for a number of years; however, the carrying costs for the vacant land and other services (mortgage, taxes, architects fees, etc.) were depleting the Building Fund Reserves. Finally, in 1978 the only option left was to sell the land at a discounted price. The JCA is alleged to have lost $45,000 on that deal. This was a bitter pill to swallow for those who had worked so valiantly to achieve this desired objective. The proceeds of the sale were used to pay off existing debts and the balance was put into a Building Fund Reserve toward the purchase of the next building. It would appear, by hindsight that these volunteers could have benefited from some professional assistance on many of these tricky issues.

Heightened Advocacy

In addition to the frantic search for a replacement building Mr. Cato had to deal with all the other issues facing the JCA, as did his predecessors.

He had to intervene on the behalf of the increasing number of immigrant arrivals. In 1975 he negotiated a merger with the Activities and Information Center, an immigrant counseling service at 913 Bathurst Street, Toronto. This provided JCA with the paid staff to better serve the growing number of clients requesting service. In 1976 the JCA presented a paper to the committee reviewing the Ontario Human Rights Act. The JCA was the only black organization to do so. Cato also obtained short-term funding from the federal government for an L.I.P. program "Attempt to Reach Others." At the end of the first term he did not seek re-election. It appeared that the failure to achieve that cherished goal, following enormous, effort was sufficient for him to call it a day. It certainly was not for lack of trying. The goals may have been set unrealistically high, so too the expectations of communal support.

Dr. Vincent D'Oyley (Part 1977)

Dr. Vincent D'Oyley assumed the presidency of the JCA in 1977 after much persuasion, prodding and solicitation. He was elected by acclamation. He was a professor of Education at the Ontario Institute for Studies in Education (OISE) at the University of Toronto and there really was no space in his schedule to take on an enormous project like the JCA.

He was really trying to do the JCA a favour to help out in a dire situation. Furthermore, there was the pending position of a professorship at the University of British Columbia (UBC). That ultimately came through and as an elite scholar he just could not refuse. He had to go. He was in the position for a mere six months and regrettably had no significant impact on the JCA.

Vincent Conville (1977-1978)

Following the departure of Dr. D'Oyley, Vincent Conville (later Dr. Vincent Conville) assumed the presidency and served for the remainder of the 1977-1978 year. These two presidents together served the first year of the three-year term. He then turned it over to Mrs. Kamala-Jean Gopie who finished out the decade to 1980. Kamala-Jean broke the gender barrier and became the first female president of the JCA. Unfortunately, she also served for only one term. The period served by these latter presidents were particularly difficult. The demands on the Association continued to be enormous and it was often a struggle to meet financial obligations. This was aggravated by having to dispose of the land on Danforth Avenue at an unattractive price. Vincent Conville states, "Let's look at the JCA and its very existence. There were days when it was Eva Smith, Neville Morrison, Jean Gopie and myself who kept the association afloat. I don't even know if Eva's family knew that the four of us floated loans to help pay off the association's debt. She put her signature on loan forms .... The very survival of the JCA today can be linked to her unselfish efforts."[14]

The financial records indicate that the Association in 1977 operated in the red to the tune of $8,232.00.[15]

JCA's First Female President
Kamala Jean Gopie (1978-1980)

The first female president took the reigns of the JCA in 1978 during a financially difficult period for the Association. Despite the hardships, the lack of funds in the financially challenged organization and other problems these two presidents (Conville and Gopie) persevered. Their presidencies were highlighted by significant interventions in the education system on behalf of Caribbean children and later other immigrant children, first in the North York Board of Education and subsequently throughout the other Boards of Education in Metropolitan Toronto and beyond. It was in the latter half of that decade (1976) that the Caribbean Outreach Program was developed with the North York Board of Education. Early drivers of this program were Monica Marsh and Eva Smith. Eva states that Monica coined the name "Caribbean Outreach Program" to enable them to better sell the program to the North York Board who were reluctant to support a program that catered to only one ethno-racial group.[16]

Monica Marsh was the chair of the JCA Education Committee and as a Social Worker with the Children's Aid Society she was able to see first-hand the difficulties being experienced by the newly arrived Caribbean children as they attempted to deal with the disorientation, and culture shock as they tried to adapt to a new country, a new culture, a new school system that did not understand them plus, in many cases, parental estrangement.

Caribbean Outreach "Booster" Program

In the school system the children were perceived to be backward and were generally placed at lower grade levels or into non-academic educational streams. To remedy this the JCA advocates, some of whom were Monica Marsh, Eva Smith, Allison Gabay, Jean Gammage-Gopie, Vincent Conville and Neville Morrison, proposed operating a "booster" after school program to upgrade the performance of Caribbean students at the Junior High School level. Subjects to be emphasized are English, Mathematics, English as a Second Language and social adjustment skills. After protracted and intense negotiation with Don Hazel, the Community Liaison Superintendent and other officials of the North York Board of Education the program was approved as an experiment.

The junior high schools selected were Don Valley, Oakdale, Jane Junior High and C. J. Parsons. These classes were staffed by Caribbean teachers who volunteered to teach these children after the regular school hours. Some of these dedicated teachers were Dave Higgins, Sheila Hoyte, Maisie Adams, Selwyn Noel, Enid Lee, Lionel Alexander, Jim Livingstone, Oscar Headley, Bernice Blackman, Randy Atkins, Jean Augustine, among others.

This program was immensely successful in helping students to properly fit and perform at the appropriate levels in the education system and thus they were able to reenter the regular stream at the appropriate level.

The Caribbean Outreach Booster program was so successful in enabling young people to become properly placed in the school system that it was adopted not only for Caribbean and black immigrant children but for other ethno-cultural groups as well—Hispanic, Italian and Vietnamese. The JCA pioneered this innovation in the school system and now it has become the norm as it has been integrated into the Summer School Program.

Saturday Morning Program

Having developed a relationship with the North York Board of Education through and with Don Hazel, the Community Relations Superintendent for the Board, Eva and the aforementioned group of advocates was able to get permission to use Oakdale Junior High School on Saturday mornings to start the "Saturday Morning Program." This was a more informal, less structured arrangement where young people, mostly from the Jane and Finch area could come and get help with their homework and assistance with subjects with which they might be struggling. They could also discuss other issues of concern to them to help them deal with racism, their ethnicity, identity and other issues that would enable them to better adapt to their new country as well as improve their grades in school. The help and assistance was provided by York, other universities students, and some high school students who were closer to their own ages and with whom they could more readily relate. It also gave the young people in the Jane and Finch community a sense of identity and self-worth as they gained confidence in themselves. This was aided tremendously by committed volunteers Bev Folkes and Linda Morowei who worked tirelessly on behalf of the JCA and the Jane-Finch Concerned Citizens Organization (JFCCO) to address the range of issues that plagued the then highly stigmatized neighbourhood.[17]

The JCA was also instrumental in another innovation in the educational system—the Language Enrichment Academic Program (LEAP).

Jamaican-Canadian Association—Executive for 1979

Front Row: (l-r) Carmen Jens, Executive-Secretary; Eva Smith, Chairperson—Education Committee; Kamala-Jean Gopie, President; Murline McDonald, Recording Secretary; Mel Thompson 1st Vice-President and Chairperson, General Purpose Committee.

Back Row: (l-r) Elizabeth Plummer, Co-Chairperson, Social Committee; Leroy Brown, Co-Chairperson, Membership Committee; Hugh Morris, Chairperson, Membership Committee; N.L. Bailey 2nd Vice-President and Social Committee Chairperson.

Missing from Photograph:—Keith Mills, Building Committee Chairperson; Jeffrey Patterson, Treasurer: Vincent Conville, Immediate Past President.

Tragic Events

Before the end of the decade of the 1970's two events occurred which grievously aggravated the black and Caribbean community, inflamed passions and prodded the community to begin to organize and to support organizations that could speak on its behalf.

The first was the fatal shooting of Buddy Evans, August 9, 1978. by a Toronto police officer during a confrontation at a Toronto night club on King Street West near Spadina Avenue. Evans was a black man from Nova Scotia. Why did police have to fatally shoot him? Could he not have been subdued by other means? This shooting brought to a head the seething resentment, even hatred, from a large segment of the black community who not only believed but actually experienced unfair, unjust and disrespectful treatment from many members of local police forces. Tensions rose and the anger of the black and Caribbean community overflowed into street demonstrations and verbal invectives against the police. The JCA had to get involved with representations, deputations and briefs presented to different levels of government and agencies thereof (police commission, City Hall, provincial government and so on). Police-community relations sunk to a new low. Racial tensions escalated during this period as many racist individuals and extremist groups felt empowered and came out to give vocal support to the police.

It would be a long and arduous task to rebuild good relations between the black community and the Toronto police. Previous attempts had been made by the police to develop better ways of policing and interacting with the non-white segments of the community. They had asked Walter Pitman, former President of Ryerson University, to study the issues that soured police-community relations and make recommendations as to how they could be resolved. The Walter Pitman Report was delivered to the police board in 1977; he listed a range of recommendations on how to make improvements. However, response to the report was slow and halting. In addition, police practices and behaviour were so deeply entrenched that it would take determined and committed leadership and stringent training and behaviour modification practices before those recommendations got transformed into altered behaviour. This did not happen by 1978 when Evans was shot; and for all intents and purposes, the community saw no visible evidence of even any intention or desire on the part of the police to change.

Dudley Laws leads marchers in protest of Police Shooting

Repeat Performance

To make matters worse and before passions had cooled, they did it again. On August 26, 1979, barely a year later, a police officer shot and killed Albert Johnson, a Jamaican, in his house in the Ossington-Davenport area of Toronto. Johnson had had previous encounters of a non-criminal nature with the police. His behaviour could be considered as unusual, nontraditional and "strange," e.g. preaching in the park and loudly reading the Bible in public and so on. Police and his neighbours were not particularly enamored with his quirky behaviours. Lots of people in Jamaica engage in quirky behaviours and they are generally humored by the populace. This type of quirky behaviour is not as readily accepted in Canada. Albert was seen by some as disturbing the peace and by others as weird and dangerous. They would rather be rid of him. Police would chase Johnson home from time to time. He would enter his house and bolt the door behind him. On August 26th two police officers who were chasing Johnson broke down the bolted door, entered the premises and shot and killed him under the pretext that they feared for the safety of others living in the house.

Another black man had been shot and killed by the police. Why did they have to kill him? Was he endangering the police officers or anyone else's life?

Could they not have subdued him, if he needed to be subdued at all, by other means? The cries of police brutality were shouted! Undue use of lethal force!! Some even shouted murder!! The JCA again came to the fore. Petitions, briefs, representations, press statements. Action needed to be taken to pacify an enraged community and to educate the police on race and gender-free policing, police-community relations and community policing.

The Cardinal is Called for Help

The government responded by again asking for eminent independent persons to come to their help and tell them what to do to avoid such tragic events. Walter Pitman had already done that in his 1977 report. They had all the answers already. His Eminence Gerrard Emmet Cardinal Carter to the rescue. He agreed to investigate and recommend ways and means to mend relations between the police and the black community. The JCA had to present another brief and make more representation even though all of this had already been done for the Walter Pitman Report in 1977.

Emergence of Black Militancy

The anger of the black community spawned the emergence of other protest groups, some of which were loosely put together to respond to the emergencies of the moment but would later just as quickly disappear. While in existence they raised the profile of the black community as they provided the bodies needed for mass demonstrations in front of the police stations, City Hall, Queen's Park and marches in the streets of Toronto. The events were led by Dudley Laws, Charlie Roach and others who some years later formalized these disparate groups into the Black Action Defense Committee (BADC). BADC under Dudley Laws leadership became a very militant and powerful voice for black and African liberation. Intercultural associations such as the Urban Alliance on Race Relations (1975) became established to focus on race relations issues and also to focus on Research and Policy on race relations. Other ethno cultural groups, such as the Chinese Canadian National Council (1980) who were also experiencing stigmatization, and racism in its various forms, began to emerge. Other ethno-cultural groups also blossomed.

Mel Thompson Returns to Help (1980-1981)

By the end of 1979 the JCA had had four presidents in three years. The organization was aching for some stability. It was the end of the decade of the 1970's and it was time to launch into the decade of the 1980's. Mel Thompson was the First Vice-President and upon the demitting of office by Ms Gopie it naturally fell to him to take the reigns to pilot the association into the 1980's. He had been there before at the start of the previous decade and here he is again to start another decade. It cannot be too strongly emphasized the devotion, commitment, loyalty and community mindedness exhibited by this man over the years. When called upon he always responded. It was not a glamorous job. The association was not loaded with money.

Indeed, quite the opposite, it was literally poverty stricken—broke.

There were no perks attached to the position. Yet it was the only organization with the profile to tackle the issues facing the black and Caribbean community. Other organizations such as the Black Action Defense Committee (BADC) (1988) and the Urban Alliance on Race Relations (1975) were yet to emerge with a credible voice to shout out against rampant injustices against immigrants and non-white peoples. The National Black Coalition of Canada was in existence but seemed not to have issues of concern to the immigrant community on their agenda and the nascent Caribbean Alliance Council had not yet emerged as a credible force in the community.

Caribbean Outreach Project

A glance at the immigration data Table I, Chart I (Appendix 1) reveals that the inflow of Jamaicans and other Caribbean immigrants peaked in the years 1973 through to 1977, with 1974 being the highest year. These numbers placed undue strain upon the meager resources available to serve them. The ensuing problems manifested themselves most pronouncedly in neighborhoods like Jane and Finch and others. This called for major remedial efforts. In 1980 Mel Thompson, Rupert James, and others in the JCA were instrumental in setting up the Jane-Finch Caribbean Outreach Service with limited project funding from the Ontario government. This program some years later became permanent as the Caribbean Youth and Family Services.

Mel Thompson remained constant through the entire period from the origin of the association until he retired following the Annual General Meeting of the Association in 1981. He did return to again serve as First Vice President in 1992. He kept the JCA's name alive. He fought the battles that needed to be fought. He persevered through the dark days until a transition could occur to better times. Then he did not stay around to share any of the glory that may have accrued subsequently. The Jamaican community owes him a very large debt of gratitude.

While I have emphasized Mel's role there are countless others who have served on the JCA Executive and its various committees through the years. They too served with valor and distinction. I should list them all but the records are so incomplete that more would be omitted than listed. I might still try to do so in an appendix, even though it would be incomplete. (See Appendix 6) but please do not be offended if you do not see your name.)

"At JCA Picnic—When They Were Young"

Part 3

The Decade of the 80's (1980-1990)

Enter the 1980's—New Blood, New Vision

We were more than happy to see the end of the tumultuous and turbulent 1970's. During the latter half of the decade the JCA had five (5) presidents in 5 years (1975-1980); and in the period 1971 to 1980 the JCA had moved six (6) times—29 Colborne Street, 65 Dawes Road, 200 O'Connor Drive, 253 Danforth Road, 984 Pape Avenue and 2400 Dufferin Street. There were two fatal police shootings but we got through it. We survived. Thanks to a faithful and hardy bunch, and resolute, forthright leaders.

Rupert James (1981-1984)

Rupert James became president of the JCA in early 1981 and served one term ending in early 1984. Rupert's background and curriculum vitae was quite different from most of the previous presidents who were (Cato excepted) mostly all academics from the educational sector. Rupert came from the social work, social services sector. He had experience and knowledge of the sector and its systems. He had served at least one term as second Vice President on the JCA Executive and as an at-large member in the second year of Cato's regime. It does not appear that he served on any of its committees. As such he would not have experienced many of the frustrations dealing with a resource-poor organization that was responding to a high demand for a variety of services. He was reasonably fresh and not yet subject to burnout, the bane of high stress situations.

As regards to Rupert's personality he was extroverted, ebullient and gregarious. He always had a smile on his face. He was easy-going and approachable. He easily identified with the so-called "common man." At the same time he claimed to be a personal friend of every politician at every level of government and in each of the political parties. He was not hesitant when introducing a cabinet minister to refer to him or her as "My Friend" the Hon. Mr./Ms So and So. He really could "walk with kings and yet not lose the common touch." He did not have the professorial aura. He would more easily be identified with the marketing and salesperson type. All in all he brought a fresh and open approach to the JCA, both internally and externally.

In Rupert's term the emphasis would definitely be placed on social services and obtaining the necessary funds from government and other sources to support them. It was strongly felt in some circles that the black and Caribbean community had been neglected by government. The other communities that had immigrants to help and service were being funded, e.g. the Italian and the Jewish communities were very well funded. The black community was not.

Rupert had knowledge of these organizations and that they had access to funds. He felt that the JCA should also be funded for all the work that was being done by volunteers for free. He also was knowledgeable of the application process. The JCA and the black community in general was practically ignorant of this whole process of accessing government funds and even that they were entitled to do so. Furthermore they lacked the political clout to demand their entitlement.

Search for Funding

The initiative for funding had already been started under the previous regime. Mel Thompson's final report for 1980 states "Special projects provided by grants from the government, e.g. the Summer Program which employed three workers; the Primary Prevention Program in the Jane-Finch area, the Co-ordinator Bev Folkes and a staff of two. The program is subject to ongoing evaluation." . . . . "The president expressed appreciation to the federal and in particular the government of Ontario for grants and support in carrying out our programs." Also "The committee successfully ran two youth summer projects. The projects were financed by the Job Creation section of Canada Manpower/Immigration Department...."[18.] This then seem to establish that 1979-1980 was the very first year in which the JCA received government funding of any consequence. That, by the way, was a mere pittance. (Former president Cato reports 1975 to be the first year that the JCA received short-term funding for a L.I.P. program "Attempt to Reach Others"[19].

The figures on the table below were prepared from the Treasurers report 1981. They show the total monies received from Government in each year for both the services already rendered and those not yet rendered. They showed that Government funding received in 1981 was almost three times less than that received in 1980. One would have expected funds would be increased in the following year. They actually decreased by approximately $40,000.00.

Government Grants Received 1980-1981

	1980	**1981**
Government Grants received	$12,383.00	$10,128.00
Advances—Education and Culture	2,060.00	1,389.00
Advances—Support and Preventative	39,739.00	15,268.00
	$54,182.00	$26,735.00
Advances—JCA Co-ordinator	5,535.00	-6,085.00
Total =	$59,716.00	$20,650.00

The report also states New Development "The appointment of Mrs. Eva Smith as Office Co-ordinator was made possible through a grant from the Ministry of Culture and Recreation," and finally the treasurer states "You will notice that our cash reserves have increased more than 150 per cent with an increase in net income slightly less than 50 per cent noting also that the Association's net worth has only increased by 37 per cent. This is because our main thrust this year was in the area of **soliciting government funding** from the various projects. However, because these grants had specific conditions attached to them these liabilities cannot be shown as equity." This simply means that the JCA had received funds in advance for services yet to be performed. To be perfectly accurate, however, there was a small grant of $8,737.53 that was received in 1979.[20] Suffice it to say that beginning around 1975 the JCA began to receive occasional, totally inadequate, grants for short-term projects.

Government had not yet committed to the JCA and/or the black community. Rupert's inside knowledge began to change this. In 1981 only $20,650 was received from all government sources. By 1982 this had become $160,829 by 1983 $214,565 and by 1984 $166,686. This was indeed a seismic change for JCA finances.

The treasurer's report shows receipt from membership dues was $852.00 in 1980 and $787.00 in 1979. Membership fee was $5.00 per member per annum. A simple division by 5 would show a paid membership of 170 and 157 respectively in years 1980 and 1979. This establishes that a relatively small group of paid up members formed the backbone of this powerfully vocal and influential but financially strapped organization.

Rupert James Innovations

Rupert James term in office was characterized by innovations. He was the one who in 1982 negotiated with The City of Toronto to have the Jamaica flag flown in the month of August for a full week at City Hall. This would be hosted at an official Flag-Raising Ceremony on Jamaica's Independence Day each year. This established a tradition which continues to this day. Many Jamaicans look forward to the ceremonial occurrence each Independence Day. He was the one who inaugurated the Senior Citizens' Dinner on Sunday, November 14, 1982 at the Grant AME Church. This has been continued every year since then and is eagerly anticipated and enjoyed by an increasing number of seniors each September.

The spring and summer of 1981 saw the occurrence of Jamaica Fest '81. This was a series of talent shows for youth and young performers across the entire performing arts spectrum to enable them to perform and expose their talents. This was an artistic success but was not repeated due to the prohibitive costs. A few successful careers were launched from this effort. A 3-day province-wide conference of Jamaicans and Jamaican Organizations was held in January 1982. It was the first of its kind and was titled "Jamaicans in Ontario; a place to live and grow." An outcome of the conference was the creation of the Jamaica-School-A-Child Project which was designed to aid primary school children in Jamaica. This project, unfortunately, did not survive. Fortunately the concept was revived and made to blossom by PACE (Canada) which was founded by Dr. Mavis Burke in 1987. The year 1981 ended on a high note as the JCA had the privilege of hosting the Prime Minister of Jamaica, the Honorable Edward Seaga. Rupert James' period in office and his initiatives began to again give a lift to the JCA's community profile.

Jamaica Independence Church Service

Another JCA initiative in Jamaicans celebrating independence was the inauguration of a Thanksgiving Church Service. Jamaicans for the most part are quite religious. Church going and worship of the Diety is deeply ingrained in the culture. Just about every known religion is represented throughout the island. Many of these religious groups founded primary and secondary schools long before the government took any responsibility for educating the country's children. It was therefore not surprising that the Jamaican citizenry in Toronto and Ontario would desire to have a service of worship and thanksgiving for their island home. They wanted to give thanks for their island's independence; their country's government; for its leaders; and for prosperity and the general well being of its people.

One of the first Thanksgiving Church Services on record was on the eight anniversary of Jamaica's Independence and was held on Sunday, August 2nd, 1970 at St. Michael and All Angels Anglican Church on St. Clair Ave., in Toronto. At that service there was the usual hymns, welcome and invitation to prayer and thanksgiving, lesson and address by the Acting High Commissioner for Jamaica, lesson read by the President of the Jamaican Canadian Association, Mr. Mel Thompson. The address was by the Reverend L. B. Harrison of St. Cutbert's Church in Oakville. The Canadian and Jamaican National Anthems were then sung followed by prayers and blessings by the Bishop of Toronto.

The Consul General to Toronto thought this was a perfect vehicle to involve the wider Jamaican community and in 1983 the planning committee for the church service, chaired by the Consul General consisted of representatives from other groups in addition to the JCA. This was the 21st Anniversary of Jamaican's Independence and it was going to be special. The service was held at the prestigious Church of St. Paul, on Bloor Street East on July 31, 1983. The crème de creme of Toronto's, and Ontario's Jamaican society was in attendance and the service was conducted with high pomp and ceremony in he Anglican tradition. Renowned Jamaican contralto Joyce Britton, sang "Hallelujah" by Mozart, High Commissioner His Excellency, Leslie Wilson did the Old Testament reading and later the Welcome. The New Testament Reading was done by the Hon. Dr. Neville Gallimore, Minister of State, Ministry of Foreign Affairs. There were greetings from the Bishops Rt. Rev'd Arthur Brown, (Diocese of Toronto) and The Most Rev'd L. A. Burke, S.J. (Diocese of Nassau). The sermon was by Rev'd Canon L. B. Harrison and the blessing was by the

Rt. Rev'd Arthur Brown. There were musical performances by the Heritage Singers and Solo by Miss Norma Phillips. There was a trumpet fanfare followed by the Jamaican National Anthem, led by Mr. Rudolf Comacho and the Canadian National Anthem led by the Heritage Singers. An organ postlude accompanied the exit of the official party. The participating clergy consisted of two Anglicans, one Roman Catholic, one Baptist, one Pentecostal and one United Church. It was truly ecumenical. Ushers were from the Commonwealth Sports Club. There was a very large turnout of Jamaicans and friends.

The Thanksgiving Services were held annually but may have been missed for some years. In the late 1980's during the conduct of one of JCA's committee meetings Hyacinth Wilson, Raphaelita Walker, Sadie Harrison, Hermine Johnson, and others decided that this tradition should be revived. They contacted the Consul General to Toronto, Mrs. Kay Baxter, who lauded the idea and advised them to proceed with the arrangements with her blessing. They contacted the Reverend Canon John Erb at St. Michael's and All Angels Anglican church who heartily welcomed their return. His congregation is comprised of quite a number of Jamaicans and the Annual Thanksgiving service was revived.

This church service of note was the 27th Anniversary Thanksgiving Service on August 27, 1989. The Rev. Canon John Erb gave the welcome. His Excellency H. Dale Anderson, brought the Prime Minister's message, Ms Joyce Britton sang the Lord's Prayer followed by the reading by Consul General, Kay Baxter. Roy Williams did the Old Testament Reading, Nehemiah Bailey did the New Testament reading. Sparkling cultural performances were rendered by Ambassador the Hon. Louise-Bennett-Coverly, O.J., the National Dance Theatre Company of Jamaica and a drum selection by renowned jazz drummer Marjorie Whylie, sister of the late Dwight Whylie. The sermon was by Rev'd Oliver Daley, Intercessions were done by Marguerita St. Juste and the prayer for Peace was by Rev. Audley James. A musical selection by the Revival Time Tabernacle Youth Choir was followed by the prayer for Our Country by Dr. Mavis Burke.

In later years coinciding with the transformation of the Black Community's religious practices the Thanksgiving Service gradually moved away from the Anglican churches toward the Pentecostal churches such as Faith Sanctuary and the Revival Time Tabernacle that are large enough to hold a sizeable congregation. In 1999 for the opening of the new JCA

Centre the Thanksgiving service was held in that building. It was held at the JCA Centre again on the 40th Anniversary.

The JCA membership has become increasingly concerned that its involvement with this activity is being diminished as the Jamaican Consulate becomes more assertive in community activities. The Membership takes pride in issues which it helped to initiate and develop and desires to continue to be a major player in these events as its position in the community warrants.

The JCA's Annual Celebration of Jamaica's Independence and the anniversary of the founding of the Association traditionally consists of three principal activities, namely the Flag Raising Ceremony at City Hall followed by the Thanksgiving Church Service and culminating with the Gala Independence Dinner and Dance, all on the first or second weekend in August.

Independence Flag raising at Toronto City Hall

TORONTO (circa 1970's-1980's)

Much had changed since the bleak, foreboding, cold, closed and unwelcoming era of the 1950's-1960's. Governments at the federal, provincial and municipal levels had changed. Social attitudes had changed somewhat, aided by legislation, public policy and public pressure.

Federal

Prime Minister John Diefenbaker (1957-1963), a staunch advocate for equality and anti discrimination announced the Canadian Bill of Rights on July 01, 1960. This was intended to guarantee fundamental freedoms for all Canadians. The preamble to the Bill declared that "Canada rejected discrimination by reason of race, national origin, colour, religion or sex." As a consequence of the Diefenbaker-espoused anti-discrimination policy there came revised immigration regulations in 1962. "Section 31 of the new regulations made training, education and skills the main conditions for eligibility. Any suitably qualified person would now be considered on his or her own merit without regard to country of origin."[21.] Further changes to the regulations made in 1967 introduced a 'points system' for evaluating the various attributes of the intended immigrant. Finally a colour-blind immigration policy had arrived. The deputations and briefs by the Negro Citizens Association, the Jamaican-Canadian Association and others had finally paid off.

Provincial

The provincial Conservative Government in Ontario headed by Premier Leslie Frost (1949-1961) passed legislation providing penalties for racial, ethnic and gender discrimination on private property. These were contained in the Fair Employment Practices Act, 1951 and the Fair Accommodation Practices Act, 1954. In addition a mechanism for seeking redress, for administering and adjudicating continuing complaints of discrimination was the creation of the Ontario Human Rights Code in 1962 and the Ontario Human Rights Commission in 1961. Dr. Daniel G. Hill, a black United States expatriate who had himself experienced racism and discrimination while serving in the U.S. army, and who had come to Canada to complete his graduate degrees at the University of Toronto, was installed as its first Director. (He is the father of the famous singer,

Dan Hill). He served in that position for 12 years and set the tone and established the legitimacy of the anti-discrimination principles which had now become not only public policy but was in fact the law of the land. Yet there were violations which resulted in hundreds of complaints to the Commission annually. The battle had not yet been won.

Municipal

At the municipal level major structural, economic and social changes were occurring. Premier Frost had created a second level of government for the Toronto area. This new Municipality of Metropolitan Toronto amalgamated the City of Toronto and the 12 surrounding suburbs for major matters while each of the respective entities continued to retain control over local matters. The super city (Metro) was empowered to do what the separate, independent municipalities could not do by themselves. This included major capital projects which would connect the various municipalities and facilitate easy movement into and between the cities and towns.

The first chairman was Fred Gardiner who became the Super Mayor. The police forces of the various municipalities were combined to form a single Metropolitan Toronto Police Force. Expressways were built—first the Gardiner, then the Allen, then the Don Valley Parkway, the Leaside Bridge, the Eglinton Avenue east extension and similar other projects began to make the cities and towns in the region more accessible. (You could actually get to Scarborough in one day.) It really began to look like one big city. The Greater Toronto Area (GTA) had begun to emerge.

City of Toronto

At the City of Toronto level spanning the previous 40 years substantial sections of the subway system had already been completed. Continuing extensions were being worked on to complete the system to what it is today. (First the Yonge Street line to Eglinton Avenue, then gradually extending north to Finch Avenue. The Bloor line was next to be built eventually extending from Kennedy Road in the east to Kipling Avenue in the west. This was followed by the Spadina extension eventually reaching Sheppard Avenue west at Dufferin Street.)

At the provincial government level there was continuing highway construction and expansion—Highways 401, 403, 404, 407, 410. There was the GO system of transportation—GO trains and GO buses. Ontario was indeed a boom province and Toronto was at the center of it all. Housing developments were springing up everywhere—north to Aurora, Newmarket, Brampton and beyond; east to Pickering, Ajax, Whitby, Oshawa and west to Mississauga, Oakville and Hamilton. Immigrants of every stripe poured into the country in droves from everywhere. They brought their skills, their education, their energy, and their money. They settled in Ontario and fuelled the provinces economic boom. They needed houses, furniture, cars, food and clothing. They became a potent economic force. Canada had become a better place and Ontario was the jewel.

It did not happen overnight—not instantly. There were many battles that had to be fought by the JCA and others in the process and there were some still to be fought. There were rampant violations in various areas which had to be brought to the Ontario Human Rights Commission for investigation and adjudication. There was the enormous amount of testing that had been done in the 1950's and 1960's with Ruth Lor and Donna Hill under the auspices of the Toronto Joint Labour Committee to Combat Racial Intolerance. There was the continuing research and writing being done by Dr. Frances Henry and Carol Tator of York University and publication of the results of their field testing. There was the Royal Commission on Equality in Employment which submitted its report in October, 1984 attesting to the reality of discrimination experienced by members of "visible minorities."

The Urban Alliance on Race Relations came into being in 1975 and provided research, policy, workshops, seminars, publications and advocacy against racism and discrimination. In 1985, together with the Social Planning Council of Metropolitan Toronto, they published their seminal document "Who gets the work? a test of racial discrimination in employment." This work authored by Dr. Frances Henry and Effie Ginsberg conclusively proved the existence of extensive racial discrimination in Toronto against "visible minority" applicants for employment. Dr. Wilson Head of York University, another black expatriate from the United States, who inspired the formation of the Urban Alliance on Race Relations was another powerful, strong, vocal advocate for change in his research, his writings and his speeches. Wilson Brooks was another valiant warrior in this struggle for equality. Bromley Armstrong's lifetime involvement in the struggle for freedom, justice, fairness and equality is well documented elsewhere and in his own autobiography,[22] Of course there were the earlier pioneers—Donald Moore and Harry Gairey Sr.[23] who chronicled their own life experiences and should be required reading for all newcomers.[24] All in all by the late 1970's to early 1980's we had come a long, long way aided by Pierre Trudeau in his years as Prime Minister of Canada (1968-1979 and 1980-1984). He instituted the "Just Society" and produced the Charter of Rights and Freedoms within Canada's constitution. Canada had become (despite the harsh winters) a desirable place to be and to live.

Roy Williams Returns to the JCA—(1984-1989)

Roy Williams returned to the JCA in 1980 after an extended absence. He was elected to the Executive Committee soon thereafter and became quite active, as he was appointed to chair the Social Committee. This committee planned and executed many successful functions. By the end of 1983 Williams was being actively recruited to run for president at the upcoming elections in early 1984. The circumstances surrounding the election remain hazy as to whether his name was submitted by the Nominating Committee or he was nominated from the floor or who the other candidates were. Suffice it to say that in 1984 Roy Williams was elected to serve a second stint as president of the Jamaican-Canadian Association.

Williams embarked on the job with verve and boundless energy. He was determined to revive and rebuild the JCA, continuing upon the foundation already laid by previous presidents, particularly Mel Thompson and Rupert James. His stated goal was to acquire a permanent home for the JCA within his first term. He immediately started a frantic effort to seek out sites that were available and that the JCA could afford. Tribute is due to Alton Telfer who had chaired the Building Committee for many years and had raised funds by putting on dances, bazaars and bake sales. A massive campaign was launched by the Alton Telfer chaired Building Committee to raise funds for the building. It included a brochure that exhibited an artist's conception of an attractive community center on the cover. On the inside were messages about the need for the center and its potential benefits to the community. There was the inevitable appeal for funds to acquire this building. There were pledge forms for different levels of pledges. The opportunity was offered to everyone to buy one single or multiple $500 bricks or to make major donations. Here was the chance for the community members to put their money where their mouth was; to really show that they wanted to do this—and they did. The JCA had major fundraising dances. It offered the community the opportunity to lend the money to the Association in the form of Jamaican-Canadian Building Bonds bearing interest at 10 per cent per annum and repayable in five years. Many who could not make outright donations of large amounts bought these Building Bonds as an investment and everyone was repaid with interest. Some actually donated the money back to the Association at the end of the five years.

A Change of Government

By 1985 the Government of Ontario had changed. There now was a friendly Liberal Government in place, headed by Premier David Peterson. Alvin Curling, a former JCA board member, had been elected with a stunning majority in Scarborough North riding and he had been made Minister of Housing. The Jamaican community worked hard to elect Alvin and the entire Liberal crew. We were friendly to them and we expected them to be friendly to us in return. We started to cash in on our IOU's, some of which had been left over from the earlier Wintario application which had been made during Mel Thompson's tenure. The JCA made the case that we wanted the money. It got some—about $175,000 was offered. That offered money was put together with about $24,000,[25] which the JCA had in reserve for the building, plus what it was bringing in from donations and bonds. The leadership was undaunted by the usual skeptics and naysayers. The enthusiasm of the public who had wandered around in the wilderness for so many years and now so greatly desired tangible outcomes greatly inspired us.

JCA Acquires Its Home

The leadership moved boldly forward. We eventually became aware that the Croatians now wanted to sell their clubhouse at 1621 Dupont Street in the western section of Toronto as they were moving to larger quarters. We concluded a deal for the building on July 5, 1985. We made the down payment, accepted a mortgage for the balance and used whatever money that remained for renovations, decoration, furniture, fixtures, equipment and utensils. We replaced the windows and doors on the front of the building giving it a brand new face lift. We built a stage and we refurbished the kitchen. We vowed to have the building ready for its official opening to coincide with the 1985 Independence celebrations on August 9th, 1985. It was frantic, but we did it. Volunteers turned out in droves to make it happen. We scrubbed and cleaned and painted and scrubbed some more until we had it ready. We amazed ourselves.

1621 Dupont Street, Toronto

The JCA Centre housed a large banquet hall, kitchen and coat room on the first floor, a board room that doubled as a small meeting hall on the second floor and three offices on the third floor. This single event in August, 1985 revived the JCA and propelled it to new heights of acceptance, credibility and influence. The renaissance that started with Rupert James' election gathered momentum and the JCA was on its way to regaining its position as the preeminent organization within the black, African and Caribbean communities to advocate for and to champion the causes of the voiceless, the disadvantaged, the oppressed, the less privileged and those who were unfairly treated.

The Grand Opening

On August 9th, 1985 the dignitaries arrived and the public arrived in droves. Many of them didn't even bother to reserve in advance. It was a hot August day. There was no air conditioning. We were overbooked and were overcrowded. The people insisted that they had to be a part of this historic occasion. We sweltered but we were proud. Finally, we had acquired our own building—The Jamaican-Canadian Centre. In attendance was the High Commissioner for Jamaica His Excellency Leslie Wilson and Mrs. Wilson.

Other head table guests included Hon. Lincoln Alexander, M.P. former Minister of Labour; Hon. Lilly Munro, M.P.P., Minister of Citizenship and Culture; Hon. Alvin Curling, M.P.P., Minister of Housing; Hon. Tony Ruprecht, M.P.P., Minister without Portfolio in the Ministry of Citizenship; Alderman Ying Hope, representing Mayor Eggleton; His Worship, Mayor Allan Tonks, City of York and Mrs. Tonks; Miss Roxanne Cohen, Miss Caribana 1985; Mr. Byron and Mrs. Vie Carter. Mr. Oswald (Ossie) Murray, Consul General for Jamaica to Toronto was there as well as the Jamaican Mayor of Owen Sound, Ovid Jackson and the former Jamaican Mayor of Southampton, Ontario, Lloyd Hales.

Honorary Life Memberships were conferred on Hon. Alvin Curling, M.P.P., Mr. Barry Beckford, the largest donor for the building, Mayor Allan Tonks, Bromley Armstrong, John Brooks and Miss Amy Nelson.

Mr. Byron Carter was the Master of Ceremonies and there were scintillating performances by Mr. Edford Providence, piano, Mr. Ronald Chambers on the cello, Miss Averil Spence on the flute and a special concerto by Jamaican soprano Miss Joyce Britton. We then were treated to a splendid performance of music, dance and comedy by the Sudbury Afro Caribbean Association Players led by Allan and Denise Jones. It was indeed a wonderful evening. People left the building feeling overjoyed and elated. As a people they finally had something they could identify with and call their own.

The United Way Comes Aboard

FRED BECK announced the admittance of 7 new member agencies at a Press Conference held at the JCA Head Office. Seated from L-R are: Roy Williams, Fatima Filippi, Ann Golden, Paul Kafele and Jane Moore.

The United Way of Greater Toronto in 1984 offered the JCA $10,000 in project funding. This started a four-year process of induction where they would give Development Funding in each of the four years as they tutored and nurtured the Association into becoming a full-fledged United Way member agency. On April 26, 1988 with appropriate ceremony at the JCA headquarters, the JCA was officially accepted as a United Way member agency.[26.] It was only the second predominantly black organization, after Tropicana, to be accepted into United Way membership. The Black Secretariat was also accepted into United Way membership on this occasion.

What did it all mean? For one it meant a source of stable funding to hire permanent, qualified staff, chief of whom was a competent Executive Director. The JCA was fortunate to get one of the best in the person of Karl Fuller, a truly professional administrator and a true blue JCA stalwart from the get go, followed by his successor Paul Kwasi Kafele. When you are a United Way member agency you begin to gain credibility with other funding bodies who formerly would thumb their noses at you. One now had access to other funding sources. One had to apply. One had to make a case to justify the funds requested. One had to report regularly to the respective funders, and on time. By 1988 the JCA was receiving funding from the Ministry of Community and Social Services, Ministry of Citizenship, Employment and Immigration Canada, Secretary of State—Multiculturalism, Metro Toronto Social Services, and the United Way of Greater Toronto—A grand total of $114,241.00. We had made a little progress. Thanks to the interventions initiated by former president Rupert James.

The Canadian-Caribbean Youth Association

One great difficulty the JCA has always had is its inability to attract and retain young people and youth into its membership. However, our beloved Mrs. Eva Smith has always had a way with young people and they all loved her and trusted her. In 1984 a very bright and talented group of young persons were graduating from the University of Toronto and York University. They wanted to stay connected and to make a difference in the society. Mrs. Smith invited them to join the JCA. They came and looked around for a while. They, however, did not want to be submerged within the JCA. They wanted their separate identity. We indicated that they could form their own youth group and obtain affiliated membership in the JCA. Thus the Canadian-Caribbean Youth Association was formed consisting of Yasmin Aarons, Karen St. Louis, Sandra Carnegie, Paul Kwasi Kafele, Everton Cummings, Joan Grant-Cummings, Anthony Henry, Akwatu Khenti, Francis Jeffers, Bunny Minott, and others. A number of them started their careers at the JCA: Everton Cummings, Joan Grant, Paul Kwasi Kafele, Akwatu Khenti, Yasmin Aarons to name a few. Francis Jeffers served on the JCA Board for a while. They were very bright.

They sent six delegates to the National Black Youth Conference in Montreal in April, 1986—the first ever national gathering of African-Canadian youth. The conference discussed many topics of interest to young people. During the rest of 1986 they put on a Cultural Show in June, a Fashion Show and Dance in July, a Boat Cruise and Dance in August and the 2nd Annual Eva Smith Bursary in October. However, they found the JCA too stuffy and ritualistic. They did not want to be an appendage to any organization that they perceived to be archaic. Furthermore they wanted to have a more pronounced African identity. We could not even effect a step-child relationship. They left and formed their own organization—Ujamaa Young People's Association. In recognition of their respect and affection for Mrs. Eva Smith they, together with the Smith family, established a bursary in her honour which is awarded each year to a deserving student at the JCA's Annual Scholarship Awards Function.

Metro International Caravan

During the 1980's at the height of the multiculturalism fervor a reporter (or columnist) by the name of Leon Kossar with the Toronto Telegram (yes there was a Toronto Telegram also a Contrast Newspaper) conceived the idea that with the large number of cultural groups living in Metro one could literally travel the world without leaving Toronto. His idea was that rather than have only Caribana to display Caribbean culture Toronto could have many festivals simultaneously in each ethnocultural community for one week in July of each year. Each Community would display its culture in the form of music, food, drinks, artifacts, cultural regalia, dances and other forms of entertainment in their general neighbourhood.

JCA Caravan days

For that one week in July Toronto would be dotted with festivals throughout the city. Tourists would be attracted to Toronto to enjoy the festivities and Torontonians would travel from one pavilion to another to sample and enjoy the different flavours of Toronto. Each pavillion would represent a city in their former home country. One could therefore visit Kiev, Cairo, Rome, Belgrade, Port of Spain, Athens or Port Royal in one night and then visit other pavilions on another night until one had visited them all or one could return night after night to his/her favorite pavilion for all seven nights. No visa was required only a passport which was a ticket that cost about $10 and was good for multiple entries to the multiple pavilions for the entire week. Visitors would have their passports stamped at each pavilion and some would vie to see how many passport stamps they could accumulate. For $10 it was undoubtably the best entertainment bargain going.

The JCA participated for a number of years as the Port Royal Pavillion. Annually it was one of the best pavilions noted for its cuisine, bar, entertainment and hospitality. It attracted hundreds of people to the JCA Centre during Caravan. However, it was a costly event as we had to pay our entertainers whereas other pavilions had regular volunteer dance groups performing for free. In addition there was a heavy reliance on our volunteers who worked tirelessly during the period without financial compensation. The only money generating activity was the bar and food sales and a percentage of tickets (passports) sold prior to the start of Caravan. After paying our entertainers there was not a lot left for the JCA's coffers. It was discontinued. It was fun while it lasted. Caravan itself died a few years later. Some considered that for the volume of passports sold the benefits accruing to the pavilions was disproportionate.

The 25th Anniversary

Karl Fuller, His Excellency High Commissioner Dale Anderson, Roy Williams, and Hon. Alvin Curling

The year 1987 was special. It was the 25th anniversary of the birth of the Association and the independence of Jamaica. We celebrated in a big way at the Downtown Holiday Inn. The JCA Centre had already become too small to accommodate such events; besides, we were seriously handicapped by a lack of parking in the immediate environs. At the head table there were representatives from all three levels of government. The High Commissioner for Jamaica, His Excellency H. Dale Anderson was the guest speaker. Others in attendance were Dr. Anderson, wife of the High Commissioner; Mayor Art Eggleton (Toronto); Mayor Allan Tonks (York); Mayor Fergie Brown (Scarborough); Hon. Alvin Curling MPP; Paul McCrossan, MP; Hon. Dr. Louise Bennett; Mr. Eric Coverley; Mr. Bromley Armstrong and Mrs. Armstrong; Mr. Bob Rae and Mrs. Rae. The Founding Members and Past Presidents were recognized. The Honorable Minister Alvin Curling presented Special Community Awards to Erma Collins, Monica Marsh, Karl Oliver, Lloyd Perry, QC, and Charles Roach. The Public Service Award was presented to Gil Scott, Director General Multiculturalism Canada. The President's Awards to Outstanding New Members were presented to Grace Baugh, David Sinclair and Hyacinth

Wilson. Bromley Armstrong, Bernice Bailey, J. B. Campbell, Byron Carter, Violet Carter, Gladstone Hylton, Inez Hylton, Amy Nelson, Pam Powell, Alex Russell, Eva Smith and Frank Wallace were presented with 25 years Continuous Membership Certificates. Following a great meal, there were scintillating performances by the Heritage Singers and the Poetic Motion dancers who provided the evening's entertainment. The more hardy ones danced away the remaining hours of the night.

To commemorate the 25th Anniversary the JCA, with funding from the Secretary of State-Multiculturalism, published a commemorative booklet entitled "Jamaican-Canadians, A Commitment to Excellence." This booklet contained a sampling of Jamaicans in all walks of life, from all across Canada, and placed on display their commitment and continuing contributions to their new homeland.

1988—Tension and Challenges—Lester Donaldson

Three events highlighted the year 1988. On August 9, Lester Donaldson was shot and killed by the police in his home. On September 12, Hurricane Gilbert hit Jamaica with unbridled fury, and on December 8 Michael Wade Lawson was shot and killed by a Peel Region police officer. The police shootings enraged the black community to an extent previously unseen. There were marches, demonstrations, protest meetings at Toronto City Hall, at Queen's Park, at Police Headquarters and everywhere. The JCA intervened with briefs and presentations to the Government of Ontario, the City of Toronto and the Metro Toronto Police Services Board. The fury was high and the rhetoric harsh as placards denounced the police action and the police in general. There needed to be the boots on the ground and they needed to be organized into an effective, militant and permanent entity that would not melt away following the end of the crisis.

Black Action Defense Committee Formed

A number of community meetings were held at the JCA Centre, to plan the community's response to the police actions. Following a number of strategy sessions by Dudley Laws, Dari Meade, Owen Leach, Lennox Farrell and others the Black Action Defense Committee (BADC) was formed in 1988 with Dudley Laws as its Executive Director and chief spokesperson. A new leader had emerged who would use militancy, persistence, stridency and non-violent protests in the streets to get the attention of the establishment that change was needed and that change must come. "No Justice, No Peace" became the mantra.

Hurricane Gilbert

On September 12, 1988 Hurricane Gilbert hit Jamaica with enormous fury, wreaking death and destruction throughout the entire island. Immediately, Torontonians of all stripes and colours rushed to send aid and assistance to Jamaica. Jamaicans, Barbadians, Trinidadians, Guyanese and every other Caribbean person of whatever stripe came to 1621 Dupont Street to help. Our building became Operations Center, Warehouse, Distribution Center, Call Center and Command Post for "Operation Gilbert". Tractor trailers lined Dupont Street full of donated supplies of every description waiting to be unloaded, repacked and shipped by container to Jamaica. Volunteers worked the day shift and the night shift as they unloaded from the tractor trailers. They packed, reloaded, and dispatched multiple containers full of supplies to Jamaica. The JCA was most grateful for the assistance from Neville Walters and the crew from Speedfreight Forwarding Company who were experts in the shipping business.

Hurricane Gilbert Volunteers at the JCA Centre

"Out of Many, One People" was never more aptly exhibited as white Jamaicans showed up, Jewish Jamaicans showed up, Chinese Jamaicans showed up, Middle Eastern Jamaicans showed up, black Jamaicans showed up, Jamaican professionals showed up and even some rich Jamaicans showed up. It was really exciting to see the beehive of activity as Jamaicans and others worked tirelessly to help save their little country—at the Jamaican-Canadian Centre. Paul Kwasi Kafele, our Executive Director, was a tower of strength and administrative acuity through it all. Paul, Neville Walters and Roy Williams were flown to Jamaica (courtesy of the Canadian Armed Forces) to inspect the damage done and the distribution of the supplies that we had shipped.

This event again high-profiled the JCA throughout the country. The JCA was an important entity in the life of the community, indeed in the life of the city. The ownership of our building made an enormous difference.

During all of this hubbub at the JCA Centre the work in the community continued apace. Paul Kwasi Kafele had succeeded Karl Fuller who had moved on to another position elsewhere. He had an excellent staff of talented young people who were busy keeping all the programs running. We were most fortunate to have had Karl Fuller and Paul Kwasi Kafele as our first two Executive Directors. Both were very talented and both were excellent ambassadors for the JCA.

JCA Stands Against Apartheid

In the mid 1980's the JCA took a firm stand against the apartheid regime in South Africa. It participated together with other groups in several events in Toronto that protested against that regime. The JCA hosted the brunch that launched the Arts Against Apartheid Campaign. In addition the Association passed a resolution and sent it to Prime Minister Mulroney asking the Canadian Government "to impose trade embargoes and economic sanctions on that evil and unjust regime." Prime Minister Mulroney responded "we are prepared to invoke total sanctions against that country. If there is no progress in the dismantling of apartheid, our relations with South Africa may have to be severed absolutely."

In February, 1990 Nelson Mandela was eventually released after 27 years in prison. Apartheid was abolished in South Africa and that country finally joined the family of nations that practices democracy and that guarantees the individual rights and freedoms of its citizens.

Another Tragedy

Nineteen eighty-eight (1988) ended on a sour note. 17-year-old Michael Wade Lawson of Mississauga was shot and killed by a Peel Region police officer on December 8th. It was just too much for the community to take—two fatal shootings of two black men within four months of each other. The community erupted in anger once again. Marches, demonstrations, protests were the order of the day. Police-Community relations were at an all time low again. The newly organized BADC produced the boots on the street while the JCA pounded on the doors of ministers, mayors, premiers and other powers that be to insist that this madness must stop. The status quo was no longer acceptable.

BADC leads march in protest of Police Shooting

Ontario Solicitor-General Joan Smith responded to the crisis by establishing the Race Relations and Policing Task Force headed by former judge Clare Lewis. The task force was mandated to investigate police practices and procedures in Ontario and to make recommendations for improvement in police-community relations. Roy Williams, was appointed to the Police Services Board in 1987, and was seconded to the Task Force by Mrs. June Rowlands, the Chair of the Police Services Board. Former President Kamala-Jean Gopie was also a member of this task force. The Task Force travelled the length and breadth of the Province of Ontario as it received delegations and heard deputations and briefs from police forces, aboriginal peoples, various "visible minority" communities, cities, towns and various special interest groups. The Task Force presented its wide ranging report in 1989 and recommended (1) the creation of the Special Investigations Unit, (2) more diversity in Ontario Police Services (3) improved community relations (4) keeping of statistics on police use of force and other matters, dealing with recruitment, training, promotion, diversity issues, affirmative action, community relations, and civilian oversight of police forces. It was very comprehensive; and it was the last commission on police-community relations, having been preceded by the Pitman Report, the Stephen Lewis Report and the Emmett Cardinal Carter Report in previous years.

Race Relations and Employment Equity

Of all the issues with which the JCA had to deal prior to the 1980's, immigration was the thorniest and most challenging. This was under control of the Federal Government and the JCA was constantly in contact with the various Ministers of Immigration, their senior bureaucrats, as well as local immigration officers. However, by the 1980's the major battles had already been won. The Immigration Act was no longer blatantly racist as it was in the earlier period. It had become essentially color blind. Country of origin was no longer an issue. Education, skills, profession and trade were now relevant factors together with deficiencies in Canada's labor market sectors. The efforts of the Association would now be devoted to fine-tuning and would involve consultations on issues such as the total number of immigrants to be allowed annually, and the allocation among the various classes of immigrants. Reference to Appendix I illustrates the spike in West Indian (Caribbean) Immigration that occurred in the early to mid 1970's.

By the 1980's the emphasis had shifted to Multiculturalism, Race Relations Committees and Employment Equity. The Multiculturalism activities was driven from Ottawa where a Minister of State for Multiculturalism had been established and the espoused policy was that Canada would be different from the United States of America by being a mosaic rather than a melting pot. Each ethnocultural group could retain and preserve its identity and culture and still be good Canadian cititzens. As a consequence various ethnocultural groups and committees became established and the government advocated for strong interaction among and between the groups. We visited them and they visited us. We sat on various committees as we attempted to understand and respect other cultural norms, values, and behaviors. For our part we had to explain to others our values, norms, and behaviors as well. A frequent visitor and partner in those days was B'nai Brith and other Jewish organizations.

Race Relations Emphasis

Alongside multiculturalism, but even more important to the black/Caribbean Community was race relations. We had to stand up and fight the battles for equal treatment regardless of colour and race. Race discrimination and prejudice exhibited itself in so many ways and in so many places. The police force was almost entirely male and white. The school administrators and teachers, similarly were nearly all white. There were no black judges in the judiciary. Provincial and municipal offices were the same. Banks, department stores, the radio and television stations were also the same.

Canadian born black persons as well as arriving immigrants had the talent, skills and abilities to do any and all of the jobs, trades and professions. The problem was getting a foot in the door. They had a right to jobs. They had a right to proper housing. They had a right to proper treatment in public places. The Race Relations focus then was to get every institution and every establishment, public or private to remove all traces of racial and gender discrimination from its laws, policies and practices and to conduct daily activities in a color-blind and gender-free manner. This sparked the emergence of two innovations—Race Relations Committees and Race Relations Training.

Race Relations Committees sprang up everywhere. The Toronto police service, the North York Mayor, City of Toronto Mayor, the North York Board of Education, The Toronto Board of Education and many others established Race Relations Committees. These were constituted to learn about race relations and discrimination, both overt and covert, personal and institutional, conscious and unconscious. The intended outcome was the emergence of new insights, policies, practices, and behaviors from the enlightenment gained through the spirited discussions of the inter-cultural committees. It also signified management's, support and commitment to a new way of dealing with each other. The JCA and other ethnocultural groups had the large job of educating top and middle level management. There were many committees on which the JCA was represented. Race Relations training involved on-site training to each level of management utilizing workshops, seminars and role playing.

Equal Employment, Employment Equity and Diversity

This was a major issue in the 1980's and into the early 1990's. First, it is the right of every individual to obtain employment for any job for which a vacancy exists and for which he or she is suitably qualified. He/she ought not to be discriminated against due to disability, color, race, gender, religion, marital status, age or sexual orientation. The focus of the black/Caribbean Community was primarily on racial discrimination. The large majority of organizations did not have many employees of colour so-called ("visible minorities") within their establishments. The thrust then, along with the Race Relations Committees (Councils) and Race Relations Training was to increase the number of people of colour in the various establishments and who, upon application, would not be disqualified solely due to their skin color. Gradually after much advocacy, deputations and conferences, things changed as more and more establishments began to declare in their advertisements that they were an "Equal Employment" establishment, later an "Employment Equity" employer. More and more firms began to actively recruit persons of colour. They not only waited for them to show up, some went out into their communities to invite them to apply. The police services, including Metro Toronto, did an excellent job to change the composition and complexion of its service so that it could better police Toronto's diverse neighbourhoods.

As the Communities changed we strongly advocated that the workplace population be a reflection of the surrounding community. People of colour began to find employment more readily in a wide cross-section of both public and private organizations.

Employment Equity and Diversity

We vigorously fought for employment equity legislation and it included protection for "designated groups" which were most affected by employment discrimination—women, people with disabilities, aboriginal peoples and "visible minorities". Even so the battle was not yet fully won. The people from the "designated groups" tended to be bunched on the lowest rung of the organizational hierarchy. The next big push was to get them to become occupants of higher level, organizational positions. We strongly advocated for fairness in promotional opportunities as well. These employees were to have access to the same additional training, professional development, coaching and job exposure that would qualify them to enter the pool of promotable employees for future selection.

A broad-based employment equity committee lobbied the Premier of Ontario (David Peterson) to implement employment equity policy at the provincial level by setting an example in the composition of Agencies, Boards and Commissions. They too should be comprised of members from the designated groups. At a meeting at Queen's Park in February, 1987, Bromley Armstrong was pressing the Premier as to when was he going to appoint a representative from the Community to the Metro Toronto Police Services Board. The Premier said "soon, sooner than you think". Bromley was disbelieving. Within the week in February 1987 Roy Williams was appointed to the Metro Toronto Police Services Board. Bromley chided me on being quiet while he was pressuring the Premier. My resume was in the Premier's hands but he had not yet confirmed the appointment to me so I could not share anything with Bromley. Following this appointment there was a string of other appointments to Agencies, Boards and Commissions across the province and the public face of Ontario began to change, perceptibly and permanently. We now can be found in many places and in many different positions. We indeed have helped to change this province and this country.

Diversity Policy Bears Fruit

The seeds were sown for massive changes which began to bear fruit in the late 1990's and early 2000's. Changes were made in the composition of the Police Services Board (Jane Pepino, Roy Williams, Susan Eng, June Rowlands, and Father Massey Lombardi) and others began to change the face of the Board as well as its policies. Roy Williams was the first commissioner to ask the chief how many on the list of police officers for promotion, that was being presented to the Board for approval, were visible minorities and women. The then chief did not know but he promised to have such information in future. Because future promotion lists were required to provide the information as to whether visible minorities and women were being promoted, change indeed began to occur. Previously the promotion list was routinely rubber stamped by the Board, no questions asked.

Increased recruitment of visible minority and female police officers resulted. Employment equity, affirmative action and diversity policies finally paid off. Changes in the number of "visible minority" police officers created a critical mass that enabled them to form their own organization, the Association of Black Law Enforcement Officers. (ABLE) Employment equity and diversity policies, procedures and practices that ensured the promotion of qualified "visible minority" officers all the way up the ranks to the first black female Inspector in 2011, and two Deputy Chiefs of police in Metro Toronto one in 2005 and another in 2009 and a Deputy Commissioner in the Ontario Provincial Police Service in earlier years. The immense external pressure forced organizations to change internally more rapidly than they would ordinarily have done.

Roy Williams resigned as president of the JCA in early 1989, midway through his third term. He felt that he had taken the JCA through the tumultuous 1980's, that his position on the Police Services Board should not be constrained by the perception that he was committed to only the organization of which he was the president. Furthermore, there would be a smooth transition as the First Vice-President "Miah" Bailey, would move seamlessly into the president's chair and take the JCA into the 1990's. Here is a portion of Williams' farewell (final) report to the JCA in 1989.

I Now Take My Leave

"Five years ago when I became President we occupied a small two-room 2nd floor office on Dufferin Street, North of Eglinton. We had no permanent staff. We had a part-time office Co-ordinator and a project worker. Our future was uncertain. Today, as I leave this office I leave you with your own building and a mortgage which is manageable and which you could pay off quite easily if you had the will to do so. I leave you in good financial health. No massive debts—other than the mortgage. I leave you with a competent staff of eight persons in three different locations administering properly funded programs that are desperately needed by this community even more so today. I leave you as a member agency of the United Way. I leave you with high profile and high respect in the public view and with government at all levels. I leave you with an emerging Senior Citizens group. I leave you with well furnished offices with modern, electronic equipment and up-to-date techniques and procedures. I leave you with the feeling that the Society is proud and pleased with the Jamaican-Canadian Association."[27]

Participants in JCA Walkathon a few years back

Part 4

The Decade of the 90's (1990-2000)

Nehemiah Bailey 1989-1992

"Miah" Bailey took the helm from Roy Williams and moved the JCA with verve and vigour into the 1990's aided by an excellent Executive Director in Paul Kwasi Kafele. The JCA operated the Caribbean Youth and Family Services Program out of offices at 2065 Finch Avenue West, with a staff of five. Head Office (1621 Dupont Street) had a staff of 5 (Executive Director, Community Development Officer, Counsellor—Immigrant Settlement and Adaptation Services and two Administrative Staff). The Lawrence Heights Project was headed by Chris Spence (now Dr. Chris Spence, Director Toronto District School Board), and Akwatu Khenti. They created the AfroCentric Achievement Society with the expressed purpose of rescuing and empowering the youth in the neighbourhood. They also created the PAL program which attempted to link a youth with a big brother who would counsel and mentor as needed. The JCA presented and spoke to their brief before the Clare Lewis Race Relations and Policing Task Force.

The JCA maintained its representation on the Toronto Police Commission's Black Consultative Committee and continued to liaise with the Canadian Jewish Congress, B'nai Brith Jewish Association, The Black Secretariat, The Black Community Planning Committee for the United Way, the Jane-Finch Citizens Community Association, Tropicana, Harambee and others. There was a policing conference with the black community on April 27 and 28, 1990. This conference explored perceptions each held of the other, identified problems and issues that created misunderstandings on both sides and attempted to find solutions that would enable better police-community relations.

There was a bus trip to Atlantic City and Philadelphia and there were multiple workshops conducted by the General Purposes Committee. The JCA was high profile and everywhere. The renaissance that started in the early 1980's continued to build to a crescendo. However, there was one dark cloud which began to appear on the horizon. The JCA was rapidly outgrowing the building at 1621 Dupont Street. It was located in the far western end of the city. There were no parking facilities and it was already too small for major functions and the number and variety of activities taking place there on a daily basis. By the end of 1989 the balance on the mortgage was down to a mere $65,000. It was already time to start searching for a new location.

"Miah" Bailey took the JCA through the first two years of the 1990's keeping the JCA on a high profile while consolidating its funding. An example in "Miah's" words—"our presentation to United Way for our usual one-year funding was so impressive they offered an automatic two-year funding with increments for the second year." After completing three years as president of the JCA, "Miah" passed the baton on to Karl Fuller in 1992 to take the JCA through the mid 1990's.

Karl Fuller Takes the Helm (1992-1996)

Karl Fuller was a JCA veteran. He was close to being one of the founding members. He had been a member of the JCA since 1963. He had served on many committees and on the Board of Directors; and when the JCA Centre was opened in 1985, he was the first Executive Director and served in that position until 1987. In addition to being an effective administrator, he was a true blue JCA believer; and he had developed his interpersonal, managerial and diplomatic skills to a high level.

Karl continued to advance the JCA profile as he raised the level of advocacy on issues such as policing, civilian oversight of police, the special investigations unit, along with the other issues of fair and equal treatment of all people, employment equity, proper education for our children and all aspects of social justice. Karl's regime also focused on "policy development, both for the organization as a whole and in the area of staffing and program operations; and today we have in place much improved written policies and guidelines."[28] In addition, a committee chaired by Ms Erma Collins was tasked with reviewing and rearranging the by-laws.

Akwatu Khenti, hired in December, 1995, as the Executive Director, supervised a wide range of community, social services and programs that he proposed "in the coming year will provide youth and family counseling, drug abuse and crisis prevention, violence against women programs, as well as counseling for survivors, immigrant settlement, community development and public education, in a manner that integrates traditional modes of service delivery with new concerns for self sufficiency, self reliance and collaboration."[29]

Recession and Retrenchment

The social and economic climate was about to undergo drastic changes in 1995. A recession was enveloping Ontario and people were feeling its effects. Many people became unemployed; incomes declined for some and entirely disappeared for others. The Bob Rae NDP Government was defeated and Mike Harris had swept into power with his "Common Sense Revolution" slogan. His Conservative Government reversed many of the hard-won gains in social and civil rights legislation and reversed some employment equity and human rights gains. That government literally turned the clock back on some social and civil rights issues.

Funding for social programs was severely cut. The JCA suffered a seven per cent (7%) reduction in their programs in October, 1995, and others were slated to be cancelled effective December 31, 1995. This resulted in the termination of one JCA employee and the reduction to a 4-day work week for others. The cuts severely affected the Community Neighborhood Support Program in Lawrence Heights, the Child and Family Service Program and the Violence Against Women Program. Precisely at the time when there was a need for increased services in the communities those services could not be offered due to the severe reduction in funding.

Ebony Cooperative Homes Inc

The JCA had started in 1988 the process to establish a non-profit co-operative housing corporation. The quite extended process included several meetings with the Ministry of Housing; selection of a real estate consultant—Aykler & Company Realty; preparation of draft organization plan and other supporting documents; submission of the application to the Ministry of Housing; proceeding to incorporate the company; receiving the Incorporation Grant from the Ministry: meeting with the consultants to discuss various sites and other issues; and the opening of a bank account in the name of the corporation among other duties. The application was submitted in 1989 for a 1990 housing allocation. Unfortunately, they did not get an allocation for 1990. They continued to apply in subsequent years. In 1994 the application was finally approved.

The JCA had, as one of its objectives, the establishment of a seniors' residence. It had incorporated the Ebony Cooperative Homes Inc. as a place where their aging population (many of whom are single females) could enjoy their retirement years in an environment that was comfortable and ethno-culturally appropriate. The Jamaican/Caribbean/black community is one of the only ethno-specific communities that is without such a facility. The incorporation was completed and a board of directors had been selected. Unfortunately, the Conservative government's axe fell on this project as funds for cooperative housing were withdrawn. This dream died and has not been revived.

Search for New Home

Despite the change in policy toward social programs and the consequent defunding of programs, the JCA had already grown to a size where it was literally bursting at the seams; and the premises at 1621 Dupont Street could no longer contain it. As a result the decision was taken to sell the building and find new premises. Much time was spent over the years scouring the city and appraising potential new sites. Finally in September 1995, 1621 Dupont Street was sold and the JCA moved its offices to temporary quarters at 1122 Finch Avenue West, giving it time to negotiate the purchase of a new site.

Amy Nelson, Chairperson of the Building Committee, together with committee members, Alex Russell and Austin Davey engaged in an exhaustive search for a new location. They examined and rejected a number of sites that were either too pricey or did not meet the exact location requirement. Fortunately, past president Miah Bailey, a licensed real estate agent discovered and took them to a site at 995 Arrow Road in the City of North York. This was an industrial building but Amy and her group saw the potential for conversion to a suitable Community Centre, and the price was manageable. She recommended that the Board purchase that property and continued to champion its acquisition.

Conflict and Controversy

The purchase of 995 Arrow Road was not without conflict and controversy. As usual there were the doubters and naysayers who felt the JCA could not handle so large a project; that they were biting off much more than they could chew; that it was too risky a venture and the debt would be too heavy a burden to bear. There were four members of the Board who recanted their earlier affirmative vote for purchase of the building and made it clear that they were opposed to the decision even though a $20,000 deposit had already been made and would be forfeited if the deal was not completed. Amy contended that she could not go back and tell the Seniors and others that the JCA had lost $20,000 because the Board of Directors could not make a decision. By a one-vote majority saner heads prevailed. There were those, encouraged by Amy, who resolutely kept their eyes focused on the objective that enabled the negotiations to proceed to a successful conclusion. As a consequence, with the proceeds from the sale of 1621 Dupont Street and a bank loan of $368,000, 995 Arrow Road was purchased to become the new headquarters of the JCA.

President Announces Ownership

Karl Fuller, the president, proudly announced at the March 10, 1996 quarterly meeting of the Association that "the ownership of the entire building was transferred to the Jamaican-Canadian Association on March 5, 1996. He expressed profound thanks to those members of the Board who were unwavering in their commitment to make this dream come true and also appreciation was due to our members who continuously convinced the Board and gave undoubted support in what it was doing."[30]

The president elaborated further that this was not the end of the journey, rather it was just the beginning as there were substantial funds to be raised for the extensive renovations that needed to be done. There were legal hurdles to overcome; zoning changes to be made; building permit to be obtained; property tax exemptions to pursue; and architects, cost estimators and construction contractors to engage. The president informed the membership that he had made an application for a $500,000 grant from the Jobs Ontario Community Action Fund to assist with the purchase of the building but that had died with the change of government and the subsequent cancellation of that kind of funding.

The president reminded the members that they now had a collective responsibility for this project. "I therefore appeal to you to seriously consider the obligation of ownership and act now to ensure that this property is transformed to a useable state. I am aware that some of you have given generous donations, others have given pledge commitments. Use whatever method you desire; purchase a bond; support an event; give a donation. We need to see funds in the treasury,"[31] The offices were quickly moved from 1122 Finch Avenue West to 995 Arrow Road, the new headquarters of the JCA, while still in an unfinished condition.

Karl Fuller did not seek reelection in 1996. After many years serving the JCA in varied capacities he sought a well-earned retirement. Having taken the JCA through to the mid 1990's and having moved the JCA to its next level with the crowning achievement of the acquisition of the new headquarters, he was happy to pass the torch to his successor—Herman Stewart.

Herman Stewart the New Captain (1996-2001)

Up to this point the JCA had always been fortunate to find a leader that was right for the prevailing circumstances and challenges. This was again true in the case of Herman Stewart. He had been a member of the JCA for the previous 16 years and had served in various capacities—First Vice President, Chair of Education, Fundraising, General Purposes and Building Committees. He had been president of the Ebony Co-op Homes Inc. and had served on the boards of George Brown College and the Ontario Federation of Labour. He had been elected head of the 4,000-member International Ladies Garment Workers Union (ILGWU)—the first black person to hold that high a position in the union movement in Ontario. He subsequently became a Mediator with the Ontario Ministry of Labour.

Herman had always been a hard worker who set specific goals to be achieved for whatever position he occupied. He also was another true blue JCA loyalist, but taking on the JCA presidency at this time was no mean task. They needed to convert a large industrial type building (M-2 Zoning) to a habitable and functional community centre with space both for administrative offices and community services—with no money in the bank. This was a very tall order. Herman was undaunted. He set about the task with his usual energy and vigour. Clearly fundraising was at the top of his list of priorities. He therefore established a "Capital Fundraising Campaign" with Ms Kamala-Jean Gopie as its chairperson while simultaneously launching a massive "Building to Serve" Fundraising Campaign which would include car raffles and many other innovative activities.[32]

The president's stated priorities for his term in office were: (1) Fundraising (2) Completion of the Building Renovations (3) Membership Growth (4) Advocacy (5) Maintaining Strong Linkages with Other Community Organizations and (6) Implementation of the Task Force Recommendations. By the end of his second year in office the only one of the priorities not yet achieved was the building renovation and this was immediately moved to the top of the list for his second term in office (if elected).

Herman was reelected and worked hard to obtain a construction loan but the banks insisted on JCA putting up forty per cent (40%) of the total cost of the construction before they would even consider it. Thus the heavy emphasis that was needed to be placed on fundraising. He also lobbied cabinet ministers and members of Parliament to support a federal grant to assist with construction costs, but to no avail.

Fundraising, Fundraising, Fundraising

The President and Board of Directors had vowed to start renovations to the building in September, 1998 and to have it ready for its official opening on August 7, 1999. With such a tight deadline everything had to be kicked into high gear. Fundraising was going well. The 1998 car raffle netted $56,000; contributions from unions $10,575; Five major banks pledged $55,000 (one bank backed out); The Heritage Singers $1,200; The Alliance of Alumni Associations $2,000 and the Peel Guyanese Association $100. Big-hearted long time Jamaican Community supporters Denham Jolly, Delores Lawrence, Leila McKenzie and Kamala-Jean Gopie came to the table with major financial contributions. The JCA submitted an application to the Trillium Foundation for a capital grant of $75,000 and the president lobbied cabinet ministers and other MP's to support the JCA's request for financial assistance. Ms Erma Collins took charge of the "Capital Fundraising Campaign" as Ms Gopie moved on to other responsibilities. The "Building to Serve" campaign provided for pledges and Naming Opportunities ranging from Supporter $10,000 plus; Partner

$20,000 plus; Sponsor $50,000 plus; Patron $75,000 plus and Major Donor $100,000 plus. There was also the "Buy-A-Brick" campaign which had an objective of selling 10,000 bricks.

Sweat Capital

Then there were the "Work Days" when dozens of volunteers came and donated their time, skills and labour to whatever aspect of the renovations at which they were competent and able. It was the modern equivalent of the old fashioned "Digging" days or "barn building" when the entire neighbourhood turned out to build one house or one barn in one day and not unlike the modern-day Habitat for Humanity. It was not only a "work day." It was also a social happening. There was friendship, bonding, camaraderie and a *joie d'vivre* that was most inspiring. The president remarked that these "Work Days" reduced costs sufficiently to enable the JCA to stay within the budget of $886,000 that was set for the renovations. The major renovations were completed on time.

The Big Day Arrives—Ribbon Cutting at Arrow Road

Jamaican Cabinet Minister Colin Campbell,
Toronto Mayor Mel Lastman, Maria Minna And Herman Stewart
at Official opening of Jamaican-Canadian Centre

August 7, 1999 will go down in JCA history as another milestone day. That was the day with appropriate pomp and ceremony The Jamaican-Canadian Community Centre at 995 Arrow Road was officially opened. This occasion was combined with the 37th Anniversary Celebrations. Mayor Mel Lastman was there. The Hon Colin Campbell from Jamaica was there. Mr. Herman Lamont, Consul-General for Jamaica to Toronto was there as was Ms. Maria Minna MP who represented the Federal Government. Mr. Herman Stewart and other members of the official party looked on proudly as Mayor Lastman and Hon. Maria Minna, M.P. and Hon. Colin Campbell cut the ribbon to officially declare the Centre open. Greetings were received from the Prime Minister of Canada, Jean Chretien; the High Commissioner for Jamaica, His Excellency Raymond O. Wolfe; the Premier of Ontario; the Leader of the Opposition; the leader of the New Democratic Party; the Mayor of Toronto, Mel Lastman; and the Chief of Police, David Boothby.[33]

The president welcomed everyone and the evening's program proceeded in order which included the history of the JCA by Roy Williams and Karl Fuller, Introduction of Founding Members and Past Presidents, the speech by the Hon. Colin Campbell, reading of Greetings from the three levels of government, the handing out of awards and musical performances by Yannick Alwood, The Heritage Singers, The Caribbean Folk Performers, Trevor Lawrence and Dionne Young. The evening's meal consisted of Fresh Fruit Cup, Summer Salad with Raspberry Vinaigrette, Penne Pasta with Marinara Sauce, Stuffed Chicken Herb Mushroom with Red Wine Sauce, Rice and Peas, Glazed Baby Carrots, Snow Peas with Cherry Tomatoes, Rolls and Butter, Coffee and Tea, and Strawberry Swirl Cheesecake.

Everyone was there. No one wanted to miss this momentous occasion. Three awards were presented as follows: **President's Award** to Uriel Soares; **Special Award** to Ms. Lillie Johnson and **Community Service Award** to Mr. Denham Jolly. Following consumption of the sumptuous meal, the delivering of the speeches, the greetings, the awards and the entertainment the assembled group danced the evening away with high spirits, euphoria and a great feeling of satisfaction and a sense of accomplishment.

Fundraising Continues

Although the JCA Community Centre had been opened the job was not yet done. There still was a large construction loan to be repaid and a mortgage on the building to defray. The president was intent on reducing these debts. The "Capital Fundraising Campaign" brought in substantial contributions from Motorola Corporation, Western Union, The United African Improvement Association and The Patty Palace. The Merritone Dances and Bonononooos Brunches totaled $55,000 over two years; "Buy-A-Brick" campaign $65,000; car raffle $90,000 and there were other events and activities taking place. The president made sure that whenever money came in it was applied to the reduction of the construction loan.

Advocacy

Busy as he was with the renovation and opening of the building the president never forgot the JCA's advocacy role. In 1997 he met with the Solicitor-General of Ontario to discuss policing. Subsequently the government appointed former Judge George Adams to review the relationship between the police and the Special Investigation Unit. He then met with Judge Adams and made recommendations. The JCA made presentations to the Metro Toronto Police Services Board on the issue of police accountability. The JCA strongly opposed the appointment of the new Chairman of the Police Services Board; however, the president met with the new chairman and brought the community's concerns to his attention. Following this a Town Hall meeting was arranged at which Mr. Norm Gardner was the guest speaker.

For the municipal elections held that year the JCA sponsored a mayoralty debate and hosted an all-candidates debate at the Centre. The JCA, together with the Congress of Black Women and the African Canadian Legal Clinic, launched a Supreme Court challenge to Canada's immigration law, and the president met with MPP Dalton McGuinty, the then Leader of the Opposition, to explore the possibility of reestablishing a JCA credit union.

In 1998 the JCA made presentations to the Toronto District School Board, the Toronto Police Services Board, the Special Investigations Unit and to the Federal Government on immigration policies. The president spoke out against the proposed bank mergers and made representation to the Children's Aid Society on a number of issues.

In 1999 the president and the vice-president met with the new police chief to apprise him of the community's concerns regarding policing. Following this a successful Town Hall meeting was organized at which they got superb print and electronic media coverage. The JCA upbraided the immigration department for offensive behaviors towards people arriving from the Caribbean as they were subjected to extensive searches and questioning that was not extended to other passengers. In addition the president was called upon continually to deal with many individual cases where he needed to intervene on behalf of persons who were being unjustly and unfairly treated by the system (public or private).

In 2001 Herman Stewart decided his task was complete. He would not seek re-election. He and his successive boards and various committees had successfully shepherded the JCA through a most difficult period in its development. There were many tricky issues to deal with involving politicians, bureaucrats, the system, the membership and the public. They were able to deftly stickhandle their way through them all. They had completed the renovation of the building. They had raised money from the members and the public. They had advocated continuously on behalf of the community and its members, and they had increased the membership in the Association. The JCA was on a high note of public acceptance and recognition. This president had brought the Association to the end of the 1990's and into the threshold of the 21st century. In his own words "it is now time to pass the torch and I do so with pride and joy. I am proud because I was given the opportunity to lead the biggest and best black community organization. For me it was an honor. I feel a sense of joy because during my time as leader the organization overcame many obstacles and struggles and achieved success and growth. To everyone, thank you."[34]

Board of Directors 1999

(Front, left to right) Uriel Soares, Maxine Adams, Pam Powell, Vincent Conville
(Back, left to right) Ruth Morris, Valarie Steele, Hector Gray, Ansel Bather, Herman Stewart, *President*, Haari Abou Korrat, *Executive Director*
(Missing) Francella Moore, Pat Williams, Claudette Cameron-Stewart

Part 5

The First Decade of the New Century (2000-2010)

A new century had started. A new decade to be travelled. A new era for the Jamaican-Canadian Association (JCA) which seems to be destined as the decade and probably the century of the woman. For 37 of the 39 years prior to 2001, the JCA had been led by men. In those 39 years only one woman had led the association and only for two years. Kamala-Jean Gopie was the sole pioneering woman. Now this was about to change. The JCA had exhausted the cadre of competent and willing men (some of whom had been recycled at least once) who were capable of leading an organization of this magnitude, influence and responsibility, or perhaps the JCA had matured, along with the rest of the society, and was now willing to support a female president. Regardless, it was now time for the women to step up to the plate after being in the background and playing a supporting role for so long.

Enter Valarie Steele (2001-2004)

Valarie Steele, a business woman who later became an Adjudicator with the Ontario Rental Housing Tribunal, had been the vice-president in 1999 and 2000. She succeeded in May of 2001 to the presidency to complete Mr. Stewart's unfinished term and then was elected to serve a full term. Her task primarily was to build upon the strong foundation left by the outgoing executive of which she was a part. The building had been acquired, refurbished and occupied. The JCA was enjoying a high level of acceptance and influence. The task then was to maintain the status quo and to enhance that position where possible. There also was the task of stabilizing and improving the operation of the Caribbean Youth and Family Service, the social service division of the JCA, which seemed to be in a state of arrested development due to an unduly high turnover of executive directors and staff members.

Youth Violence Initiative

An early challenge for Valarie Steele's administration was to address and possibly stem the escalation of youth violence which was sweeping across the city and had become a plague to various communities. There was too much involvement of young black men in gangs who dealt in illicit drugs and had violent encounters resulting in shootings and deaths. Hardly a weekend went by without an incident resulting in the death of another black youth. To address this issue, the JCA initiated the Youth Violence Initiative Project which resulted in the Conference on Black Youth Violence "to work for elimination of the causes and search for cures for the malady."[35] The objectives of the Conference:

1—To explore with our youth the causes of violence, the emotions associated with violence—as perpetrator and as victim—and increase their awareness of the cost (personal and societal) of violent behavior.
2—To explore approaches for behavior modification and improvements in parenting, teaching, guiding, counseling, policing and employment of black youth to reduce the impulse to violence.
3—To involve youth, parents, teachers, youth organizations, social workers, the police and justice system, business and the wider community in a search for lasting solutions to the issue of youth violence in the Black Community.

In further pursuit for a solution of this virulent problem the JCA joined with other organizations to establish the **"Building Hope Coalition."** This coalition met with police, the residents of the affected neighbourhoods, and other community groups and had briefings at the federal, provincial and municipal levels. Federal Member of Parliament, Hon. Jean Augustine, used her good offices "to convene a meeting of the "Coalition" with Federal Government officials to address some of the issues they felt were extremely important to the uplifting of the Black Community."[36]

Follow up to UN World Conference

The JCA responded to the United Nations World Conference Against Racism, Racial Discrimination, Xenophobia and Related Injustices held in Durban, South Africa in 2001 by developing and delivering a three-part lecture series on the issues:

1—Post Durban, Where do we go from Here?
2—How Racism Affects Health and
3—The Prison Industrial Complex, the Criminalization of a Race.

The president explained "The JCA reparations lecture series is designed to educate the African Canadian community about this history and the consequence and multi-faceted challenge faced by our communities to understand the primary causes of our condition, as well as the urgent call to defend our interest."[37]

40 Years of Caring and Sharing

The highlight of year 2002 was the 40th Anniversary celebrations of the formation of the JCA and the anniversary of the independence of Jamaica. The slogan "40 Years Caring and Sharing" was selected for its marketing and publicity campaigns. A 40th anniversary fundraising target of $40.00 per member totaling $40,000 was set to enable a celebratory reduction of the mortgage on the building in the 40th year. The planning committee produced a commemorative video highlighting the surviving "Founding Members" and their reminiscences about the conditions in the early days and paying tribute to the deceased members: Esmund S. Ricketts, George King, Ira Dundas, and Owen Tennyson. An impressive 40th Anniversary Service of Thanksgiving was conducted at the JCA Centre on August 4, 2002. The sermon was given by Dr. Pat Francis of the Deeper Life Christian Ministries. Other officiating clergy were: the Rev. Aldith Baker (St. Wilfrid's Anglican Church), Rev. Dr. Audley James (Revivaltime Tabernacle), and Archbishop Dr. Delores Seiveright (Shouters National Evangelical Spiritual Baptist Church).

The Independence Gala Programme was a grand affair. Messages were received from the Governor-General of Jamaica, the Prime Minister of Canada, the Prime Minister of Jamaica, the Leader of the Opposition in Jamaica, the Premier of Ontario, the Leader of the Opposition in Ontario, the Mayors of Toronto and Mississauga, the High Commissioner for Jamaica and the Consul General for Jamaica to Toronto, the Chairperson of the United Way and several Members of Parliament and of the Ontario Provincial Legislature. It was a star-studded array of dignitaries and message senders. The team of Jones and Jones was the MC for the programme which consisted of the JCA president's address followed by prayer, followed by dinner, and the reading of the greetings. Ms Vivia Betton, the Consul general for Jamaica to Toronto, introduced the Guest speaker, the Hon. K. D. Knight, Jamaica's Minister of Foreign Affairs and Foreign Trade. The Vote of Thanks to the Guest Speaker was given by JCA vice-president Claudette Cameron-Stewart followed by the presentation of Honours and Awards, the video presentation of the founders, entertainment, vote of thanks and the closing remarks. The evening was topped off by dancing to DJ Al's Supernatural Disco.

The 40th Anniversary Honours and Awards were:

> **President's Award**—Maxine Adams and Adaoma Patterson
> **25-Year Continuous Membership**—Theo Briscoe and Barbara Thomas
> **40-Year Continuous Membership**—Bromley Armstrong, Bernice Bailey, Byron Carter, Violet Carter, Inez Hylton, Gladstone Hylton, Amy Nelson, Beryl Nugent, Pamela Powell, Melbourne Thompson and Frank Wallace. **Lifetime Membership**—Gladstone Hylton, Carmen Jens,
> **40th Year Anniversary Pins**—To Founding Members and to Past Presidents Karl Fuller and Herman Stewart. **2002 Community Award**—Neville Walters

Standing Together Against Racial Profiling

The JCA and many organizations within the Black Community stood together in support of the series of articles published by the *Toronto Star*, June, December, 2003 on Racial Profiling by the police services. They met on a monthly basis. They met with MPP Dalton McGuinty, leader of the

Mr. Honderich (above, center) was photographed with prominent members of the community including Valarie Steele and Herman Stewart, president and vice president of the JCA respectively.

Opposition, and attempted to meet with Premier Ernie Eves to discuss the matter and seek legislation to outlaw the practice. They also met with the vice-president and the case manager of the Ontario Civilian Commission on Polices Services (OCCPS) and left feeling that positive outcome would result. The JCA showed its appreciation to the *Toronto Star* by honoring its outgoing publisher John Honderich at a reception held at the JCA on May 24, 2004. This reception was attended by a large cross-section of the black Community who turned out to express their appreciation for Mr. Honderich's courageous decision to publish these articles which certainly would earn him and the *Toronto Star* the ire of the police establishment. Mr. Honderich was presented with a painting by artist Phil Campbell.[38]

Scholarship and Bursary

Over the years, JCA had given scholarships to deserving students—sporadically. In 1995, under the leadership of Everton Cummings, chair of the Education Committee, the "I Have a Dream" and the Eva Smith scholarships, each for $1,000 were awarded. For lack of funds, there was a hiatus.

In 2002, Dr. Ezra Nesbeth approached the JCA and offered $20,000 to resuscitate the scholarship program. Under the leadership of Barrington Morrison, the Education Committee then kicked itself into high gear and offered 6 scholarships in 2003. The sponsors were Dr. Ezra Nesbeth, Prof. Erma Collins, the Hon. Mary Ann Chambers, the Jamaican Canadian Association and Victoria Mutual Building Society.

The Scholarship Dinner and Awards has evolved in subsequent years into one of the signature events at the JCA in the month of September. In 2011 the number of scholarships/bursaries valued at approximately $50,000 were awarded to 46 recipients. The total amount awarded between 2003 and 2011 was $210,000. Over the years many young persons have been aided as they pursued their higher education goals. This is a most rewarding activity and members and others are invited to make contributions to the existing scholarships or to fund additional scholarships to be awarded by the JCA. This is really one of the best investments one can make in our young people.

JCA Scholarship Donors and Recipients

JCA Spelling Bee Competition

Advocacy

During 2003-2004 considerable advocacy efforts were initiated by the president and vice-president who, together with other community leaders, met with the federal Attorney General to discuss changes to the Criminal Code, gun violence, drug trafficking and an affirmative action program for the criminal justice system. The JCA together with other organizations formed the "Coalition of the Committed" to address the continuing problem of youth gun violence, and together with the Black Action Defence Committee (BADC) conducted a town hall meeting to address the issues of policing and gun violence. The president and vice-president met with the Attorney General of Ontario to discuss these matters and to urge him to quickly implement the recommendations of Commissioner Judge LeSarge regarding civilian oversight of police officers. They also met with Mr. Allan Heisey, the new chair of the Toronto Police Services Board to apprise him of the communities' concerns with regard to police-community relations and police oversight. They, together with other community organizations, met with MPP Dalton McGuinty who was the Leader of the Opposition; but it was expected that he would soon become Premier and would be in a position to positively address policing issues in Ontario. The JCA might be characterized during this period as having a heavy emphasis on "blackness," black racism, and on black anti-racism issues.

David Griffiths (2004-2005)

At the end of her term as president Ms Steele was not re-elected. Mr. David Griffiths was presented for election by the nominations committee, and was elected. The Association was both enthused and optimistic as Mr. Griffiths was a fresh face and from a younger demographic group. They hoped that his presence as president would be a magnet to attract a significant number of that demographic group into the association. The JCA had always struggled to attract and retain younger people.

Mr. Griffiths graduated in 2000 from the University of Windsor with a Bachelor's degree in Industrial and Manufacturing Systems Engineering and had held positions with Nortel Networks and Symcor. He was an engineer trained to think and act logically and systematically.

He had served one term on JCA's board as chairperson of the Youth Affairs Committee. It appears that he had influence with a group of young men and young women whom he encouraged to join the JCA. This group he apparently considered to be his constituents and they would be the catalyst that would breathe new life into and change the JCA into a new image. In effect the Youth Affairs Committee was structured to mirror the Association's Executive Committee with himself as chairperson, and other positions being Associate Chair, Public Relations Officer, two Event Co-ordinators, Secretary-Treasurer, Membership and Community Liaison Advocate. The former president Ms Steele remarks that "from his first JCA board meeting he indicated to the Board that he wanted to have his own bank account, and wanted to know if the JCA had set aside money for the group to operate. The previous treasurer and I explained to him that that is not how JCA works and walked him through the way we do business. He was displeased and continues to be displeased."[39]

The Youth Affairs Committee's report contained an elaborate agenda of activities to be accomplished during his term as chairperson, chief of which was the Young Professionals Gala which occurred in November, 2002 and which was an artistic success. However, all the JCA rules for receiving and depositing cash, the payment of bills and the prompt delivery of money to the treasurer were violated.[40] This behavior clearly deviated from established practices and was observable at an early stage and reported at a quarterly meeting. Mr. Griffiths approach and line of thinking differed from the rest of the board members. Still he was elected president. In less than a year he resigned. The culture clash was too formidable. In his mailed-in President's report he remarks:

"From the past year we are reminded of the persistent infinity of transformation. We are reminded too, that transformation occurs for a reason. Some changes are more challenging than others. Regardless of the outcome, we have survived as an association and as a community. We are also reminded that we cannot prosper or even survive if we do not engage in a transformational process."[41]

Transformation is a process indeed. It is not an event. It takes time and it cannot be imposed and it does not occur instantly. It has to be carefully crafted.

It was quite unfortunate that the JCA lost an individual like Mr. Griffiths, young educated, enthusiastic. But like the CCYA back in 1986 the young, university-educated population are action-oriented, needs to be engaged with tangible outcomes that are achievable in a relatively short time horizon. Furthermore, the engineer's mind is programmed in favor of systems and precision and does not readily accommodate imprecision, temporizing, indecision and undue delay that impedes the achievement of objectives. In addition the high achievement motivated individual cannot function in an environment where he/she does not have direct impact on the desired outcomes. The culture clash was inevitable.

The resignation of the president resulted in a temporary disarray but which was quickly brought back to order by the vice-president Mr. Herman Stewart. Stewart together with the recently retired President, met with Commissioner, Justice LeSarge and presented the JCA's submission for the creation of a public complaints commission to deal with citizens' complaints against police. Justice LeSarge having made such a recommendation the JCA followed up by letter to the Attorney General urging him to act quickly to implement Justice LeSarge's recommendations.

During the year the JCA recruited the following staff: Executive Director, Program Director, a full-time Fundraiser and a Volunteer Co-ordinator. None of whom remained with the Association.

Sandra Carnegie-Douglas (2005-2009)

With the election of Ms. Sandra Carnegie-Douglas, the JCA resumed the decade of the woman. Sandra was no stranger to the JCA. Her first contact occurred in 1984 when she was a member of the Canadian Caribbean Youth Association, which later became the Ujamaa Young People's Association, which she served as president in 1989. She also served as a facilitator for workshops, seminars and Organization Development (OD) interventions. She joined the JCA in 1994 and became the Chairperson of the Fundraising Committee. She then became first vice-president of the JCA in 1995. She came as somewhat of a known quantity and with a positive image. Her day job was with the Metropolitan Toronto Housing Authority as a human rights officer. She had a passion for human rights and anti racist issues and had an extensive involvement in Black Community issues.

It is therefore not surprising that, right from the outset, she would get deeply involved with the intractable problem of youth violence with its weekly reports of shootings and killings of young black men. This demanded attention not only by the police but by the communities as well. This abhorrent behavior tended to stigmatize the respective communities and black people in general. Ms Carnegie-Douglas was instrumental in forming another coalition to tackle the problem. This was the Coalition of African Canadian Community Organizations ("The Coalition"). In her words:

> "The "Coalition" has generated local, national and international attention to, and dialogue on, the situation of the African Canadian community in Ontario. It has broadened the dialogue and analyses on gun violence and its root causes, and the impact on African Canadian youth, families and the community. The "Coalition" has brought national focused attention to the issue of Anti-Black racism, its systemic marginalization and exclusion of African Canadians—socially, economically, politically and culturally—conditions which breed criminal activity and gun violence."[42]

Advocacy

The JCA was fully involved through discussions with the Government of Ontario on several legislative changes. These include: The Safe Schools Act; The Ministry of the Attorney General on Bill 103—the establishment of the new Independent Civilian Review Mechanism and a new independent complaints process following the report of Judge LeSarge; and the Ministry of the Attorney General on Bill 107—to amend the Human Rights Code and reform the Ontario Human Rights Commission (OHRC). The JCA added its voice objecting to a Toronto District School Board (TDSB) trustee's attempt to eliminate Black History Month in the school system and replace it with a Heritage Month. The JCA advocated for and strongly supported the establishment of the Africentric School. The JCA in conjunction with Operation Black Vote and the Jane Finch Concerned Citizens' Organization (JFCCO) hosted an All Candidates Debate at the Jamaican Canadian Centre on the African Canadian Agenda during the 2006 federal election.

A significant accomplishment during Ms. Douglas' term was the Ontario Government's ultimate response to the advocacy by the JCA and "The Coalition" to create and fund the Youth Outreach Worker program. This program begins to focus on the problem of violent youth. The JCA was appointed lead agency for this program in the Northwest Toronto catchment area which include partner agencies Hincks-Dell Crest Centre,

Griffin Centre, PEACH Organization, Jane-Finch Family and Community Centre, Midaynta Community Services, and the Black Action Defense Committee. This was of special significance as this was the first time that a predominantly black/Caribbean agency had been granted lead agency status and responsibilities.

Organizational Transformation

The "transformation" alluded to by former president David Griffiths began to be given serious consideration by the JCA Board. It decided to initiate an organizational review and contracted the Wise Consulting Group to assist the organizational review committee to conduct the process. The rationale for the review was that the various environmental factors had changed so dramatically over the 45-year life of the organization that currently held theories, philosophies, practices and culture may no longer be appropriate. They may even be outright dysfunctional and counterproductive. For example, the heavy dependence on volunteers which had worked so well in the past may no longer be appropriate. There may very well be a need for more professional, paid personnel to effectively discharge organizational responsibilities. In the process there may be an induced detachment among the members as they are no longer involved and they lose their emotional attachment to the organization, while on the other hand the paid staff has little or no emotional commitment to the organization.

During Ms. Carnegie-Douglas tenure there was forward movement with the organizational review. New policies, protocols and practices within the Association were developed and implemented. There were major upgrades and renovation of the building and there was high visibility and advocacy on issues that impacted the constituencies served by the JCA. During this period there was a strong focus on anti-racism and anti-racist issues. She did not seek reelection.

Herman Stewart (A Brief Interlude—2009)

Herman Stewart was invited to return and was re-elected as president of the JCA; however, there were some internal conflicts that could not be easily and amicably resolved. Herman chose to resign halfway through the first year.

Flag raising ceremony at the JCA Centre

Audrey Campbell (2009-2012)

Audrey Campbell joined the JCA in 2004 and served on the Membership Committee as its vice-chairperson. She also served as a member of the Fundraising Committee. She was then elected to the Board of Directors in 2008 as the Executive Vice-President. This was in the last year of Ms. Carnegie-Douglas' term; and being relatively new to the JCA Ms Campbell was still learning the ropes. With the resignation of Herman Stewart the JCA resumed the decade of the woman as Audrey Campbell, the Executive Vice President, became the president. She was the third woman of the decade so far to do so. She succeeded to the presidency to complete Mr. Stewart's unfinished term and then was elected to serve a full term. To have the role and tasks of the presidency dropped on one's shoulders suddenly was surely an immense challenge.

Fortunately, Miss Campbell has an ebullient personality, and is highly extraverted. She has excellent interpersonal skills, is a good communicator, has excellent team-building skills, is a good delegator and is a fast learner. She was able to convert what formerly was a contentious Board into a highly cohesive, synergistic team. (Some former board members had exited) Some of the other Board members were equally new and inexperienced. To almost the entire Board there was the dual challenge of performing while still learning and striving to meet the expectations of the membership and the larger society. They undoubtedly had a few missteps, but on the whole they weathered the storm with flying colours. They could be ranked quite high on the list of the more cohesive Boards of the JCA. Any perception of the JCA in crisis was soon dispelled. The JCA was back on track. In addition this Board was young, fresh and predominantly female.

To compound the problems faced by the new president and Board, there was the responsibility to implement the proposals of the organizational review by the consultants. The consultants had offered a couple of options on the choice of an organization structure. The one selected and recommended by the Board included a General Manager's position (formerly Executive Director) with the exotic title of Chief Executive Officer who would have overall responsibility for the management of the JCA, its building and equipment, its membership services and the social service delivery operations. The CEO was newly hired in March 2009. He was totally new to the organization and was unfamiliar with its history, its culture, its traditions and the community. He too had to find his way concurrent with the Board who was also finding its way. Fortunately the multiple committees—the backbone of the JCA—discharged their functions effectively; and the staff of the Caribbean Youth and Family Services and other programs performed their appointed functions up to expectations and the JCA ship never veered off course.

As might be expected in the first year, much of the Board's energy was focused on internal matters—mending fences and cementing relationships with funders, some of whom had had cause to be annoyed with the JCA. Regular functions went ahead on schedule as the committees did their jobs. Fundraising activities—Boooononooooonos, Walkathon, Golf and the Raffle proceeded apace. The 46th Annual Independence Gala proceeded with the usual glitter and glitz. The guest speaker was the Hon. Robert Montague, Minister of State in the Office of the Prime Minister of Jamaica. The Seniors' Dinner and the Scholarship Awards Dinner were very successful and the year ended with the usual Christmas Party for the children and the Annual New Year's Eve Party.

Some time and effort was spent modernizing the computer and Information Technology systems to better track membership data, generate income tax receipts, accounting and other matters to make the management of information more efficient.

Advocacy

The JCA's strength over the years has been its ability and willingness to stand up for the rights of those who are oppressed. disenfranchised, underrepresented, unfairly and unjustly treated and to be a voice for the voiceless in our society. Justice, equity, fair treatment, anti racism, and anti discrimination are fundamental pillars on which the Association was built. It had always championed the causes of the so called underdogs. It has always been willing to speak out, loudly, against any and all infractions of and encroachment on the inalienable rights of freedom and justice for human beings, especially those of humble status. The dozens of briefs, presentations, press conferences and media interviews testify to this—but not lately.

It appears as though the voice of the JCA has been muted. Hardly has it been heard on pertinent issues of concern to the communities. The General Purposes Committee, which was the Association's watchdog on advocacy-related issues from the formation of the Association in 1962, was abolished in 1991. The amendment to the constitution was worded thus: "That the General Purposes Committee be discontinued. That the duties originally assigned to this committee be the responsibility of the paid staff who has the "expertise" to deal with them more effectively.[43] The motion passed by a vote of 26 to 11 for a total of 37 members voting at an Annual General Meeting. Twenty-six members changed the direction of the advocacy efforts of the JCA. Twenty-one years later one can judge the efficacy of that amendment. No one on the Board currently has direct responsibility for advocacy and on the staff even less so. Is there any wonder that the voice of the JCA has been muted and even worse—silenced. With the death of Dudley Laws, to whom does the community now turn to speak out on issues of their concern? One wonders whether the JCA's energies have been totally redirected toward the social services sector to the exclusion of its original purpose. This board has assigned Advocacy to a newly created 5-member Public Policy Committee (Three of whom are board members). The public policy committee's mandate is to advise the Board on emerging and or existing issues and to formulate recommended responses.[44] The question may well be asked, does the Community still need to have a collective voice? and/or is advocacy still required?

Transformation

From time to time over the years, the JCA Board, Senior Staff and Committee Chairs would go off site for a weekend retreat to engage in Organizational Development (OD) initiatives, team building and/ or strategic planning activities. Somehow the decisions taken at these retreats seem seldom or never to get translated into observable behavior or operational changes. Often this was due to the short tenure in office of each regime and the failure of the successor regime to follow through with the plans formulated by the predecessor. The next retreat two or three years later would return with similar recommendations and decisions as the former and the cycle would continue ad infinitum.

In 2009 under the urging of the United Way an extensive Strategic Planning process was undertaken. This was facilitated by an experienced OD consultant at no cost to the JCA. After working through the data collection and group discussion stages of the process the problem-resolution stage identified the critical actionable areas that needed to be addressed. They are:

1—Recruit and Retain Substantial number of New Adult Members for JCA
2—Attract and Retain Substantial number of Youth Members for JCA
3—Develop a clear Identity and Image for JCA, and
4—Develop Sources of Stable Funding for JCA on a continuing basis

Four groups were selected to work on the identified areas to achieve tangible and measureable results. As of the publication date no official measured results or interim reports have been presented on each of the areas. It is still a work in process.

New Employment Emphasis

In 2010 there was a shift in the focus of the employment services program delivered by the JCA. The Opportunity Plus Adult Employment Program had targeted the labour force demographic of unemployed persons age 45 and over to retool and reposition themselves to obtain gainful employment in an ever-changing labor market. This program assisted them in this process. However, the program was phased out by the government in 2010. The new focus is an employment service that will serve the entire spectrum of the labour force and the labour market. This new program is Employment Ontario and it is funded by the Ministry of Training, Colleges and Universities. It is a full-scale employment preparation and job search service. It includes Job Search, Job Training/Retention, Research and Information, Job Matching, Placement and Incentives, and Referrals to other programs. The JCA was selected to deliver the Employment Ontario program in the Northwest Toronto area. Funds were provided by the Ministry to refurbish the office and provide equipment to bring it up to uniform Province-wide standards.

"Members Attend Meeting at JCA"

JCA 2011 Job Fair

Some participants at JCA Employment Ontario Job Fair

Contribution
by former President Kamala-Jean Gopie (formerly Jean Gammage)
for the Jamaican Canadian Association, 1962-2012

I joined the JCA in 1975 or 76. I was an educator who was concerned about the experiences of Caribbean immigrant children in the school system. As a result of asking around, I found out about the JCA and volunteered in 1975 to provide after-school help to students at Jane Junior High School.

I was President from 1978-1980, following Vincent Conville who completed Vincent D'Oyley's term (1977-1978). For the 76-77 term, I was the Executive Secretary before becoming President in 1978. After continuing on the board I chaired the Education Committee.

I was quite involved with JCA during the 70s and 80s working on the board and several committees. Then around 1996 I assumed the chair of the Capital Fundraising Committee to raise funds for the renovation at 995 Arrow Road. Before stepping down in 1998 because of conflict of interest guidelines related to my job, I was able to obtain pledges for well over $100,000.00 (including $55,000.00 from the banks).

During my time of active involvement with the JCA, we took on an advocacy role on behalf of students and worked closely with the North York Board of Education. (Eva Smith and Monica Marsh were integral to that work). As a result of our efforts, the LEAP (Learning Enrichment Academic program) was established whereby immigrants from the Caribbean got extra help both during the school day, after school and during the summer.

In 1972 (I believe) the Immigration Act changed. This enabled many women, who had migrated earlier, to bring their children from the Caribbean to join them. Thus began the large scale entry of Caribbean students into the school system. For a variety of reasons many of these children were ill prepared to integrate and succeed in the system (children had not attended school regularly back in the Caribbean so knowledge/skills level were below acceptable grade level, some mothers had difficulty relating to their children—some had not seen their children for years, some children had difficulty fitting into a new/different family and saw themselves as outsiders). Thus in 1975 when JCA began its education advocacy it was in the forefront of organizations seeking to help immigrant/minority students succeed. We would not meet only with board officials but we held Sunday afternoon parent meetings in community centres to help parents prepare for parent/teacher interviews.

During the 70s the Multicultural Policy was enacted in Parliament and this strengthened the JCA's effort to seek support from the Federal Government for the education/arts and cultural Saturday Morning Program. We also obtained support from the City of Toronto—Eva Smith did a lot of work on this. This was also a time when White Power groups were active in Toronto and so JCA worked with race relations groups to address issues of racism. By the late 70s, there were issues with policing as well (Buddy Evans, Johnson death). JCA worked with the police and Cardinal Carter to find solutions to the problematic relations between the Jamaican/black population and the police. I was on TV (Black World) to discuss our concerns.

Indeed, the 1970s was when JCA began to be more than a social/cultural organization that was only concerned with hosting events (charter flights to Jamaica, dances, dinners, picnic, hosting Jamaican diplomats and politicians, etc.) for its members. It began to see the need to provide social services which would enable Jamaican/Caribbean immigrants to integrate—e.g. housing, employment, and education. The purchase of the Dupont Street building in 1985 provided space from which a variety of programs was delivered. Over time, JCA outgrew this space and so the Arrow Road building was purchased in 1996.

JCA was in the forefront of Caribbean organizations which saw advocacy as one of its reasons for being. Often, it was the only one which gave voice to the many issues and concerns affecting the Caribbean population. As a result it developed credibility and legitimacy in the Toronto area. Meetings with the police, politicians and bureaucrats, school board personnel, B'nai Brith, etc. were convened to seek support for our efforts to deal with racism and other social service concerns which impacted Jamaican/Caribbean immigrants.

I am not sure when JCA became a member of the United Way. In any event, this would be evidence and recognition that JCA was more than a social/cultural organization. This has not been without its problems. The organization now had "two masters"—the membership and the funding agencies which support the social service programs. The focus of each was clearly different and the board had a difficult time figuring out how to manage. Board governance has generally been ineffective, which resulted in frequent turnover of Executive Directors and staff. Lack of continuity as well as the delivery of social service programs suffered, as well as JCA's reputation with the funders.

During my time of active involvement with JCA (mid 70s to mid 80s) the membership was around 500 paid members though many others would participate in the social/cultural events. However, after JCA purchased its building on Dupont Street there was some growth. Prior to that, we did not have a home after the building on Dawes Road burned down (in 1972, before my time). During my years on the board, we rented space for office on Danforth Avenue and then on Dufferin Street.

Over the years, the JCA would raise funds from events, ask for donations from members as well as seek grants for specific programs from different levels of government. The Walkathon was started when JCA was headquartered at Dufferin Street. The Golf tournament started after the move to Arrow Road. The Scholarship Fund and events have grown quite significantly over the last five years due to support from the community.

There have been problems around identity—who does JCA serve/represent—Jamaicans or the black community? Given the Jamaican motto, "out of many, one people" to call itself a black organization is divisive in that it makes some Jamaicans (e.g. those of Chinese, Indian heritage) feel unwelcomed. While most of our membership is black, we must ensure that all documents (constitution, policies, newsletters, committee reports, annual reports, flyers etc.) convey a message that is always inclusive of all Jamaicans. Also, based on the legacy of class divisions in Jamaica many professionals in our community do not see JCA as a middle class organization and so are not involved. Rather, many sit on the side lines and criticize instead of joining and helping to build and improve the organization. Accordingly, JCA has to make a concerted effort to build bridges and reach out to all sectors of the Jamaican community in the GTA.

With the upcoming 50th anniversary of Jamaica and the JCA, the organization has an opportunity to blow its horn and tell about its achievements over the years as well as set its agenda for the years to come. It needs to reach out to young people and Canadians of Jamaican heritage. Most of the founders are no longer with us and so it must look for new blood and individuals who are visionaries to assist the organization to move forward to meet the challenges of the future. Clearly the organization, in its current operation, has gone well beyond the dreams and expectations of its founders. This of course is due in part to the population size and service needs of the Jamaican population.

As someone who believes in JCA and has supported the organization in a variety of ways for the past thirty plus years, my hope is that it will indeed go from strength to strength. As we mature, we must act in a professional manner, be respectful of each other, value the contributions made by members and others, and strive always to present Jamaica and JCA in the best possible light. We have to be there to present/voice the positive picture in order to counter the negative messages so often seen in the media.

In spite of the shortcomings, the JCA has a legacy of advocacy, providing services to meet the needs of an immigrant population, as well as being a place where groups can meet to celebrate our heritage.

The contributions of Eva Smith, Monica Marsh and Rupert James are particularly significant since they were the visionaries who moved JCA beyond its social/culture focus.

Students at the JCA Saturday Morning Tutorial Program

JCA Scholarship Committee Members

An Interview
with Former JCA President Miah Bailey—Looking Back
Reprinted from *InFocus*, May 2003

Mr. Miah Bailey is a retired Educator and committed Community Organizer. Mr. Bailey taught school both in the Toronto District School Board as well as in Jamaica. Miah lives his motto: "Mankind cannot improve itself without improving others; selfishness is a road to destruction."

IF Please tell me about yourself.

MB I am a retired teacher/educator and I also do a reasonable amount of work in industry in the engineering field. For 38 years I have been doing voluntary community services, right here in Toronto—1964 to present.

IF Where did you teach?

MB With the former Etobicoke School Board

IF Did you teach in Jamaica as well?

MB Yes, for seven (7) years with my last school being Kingston College.

IF When did you come to Canada?

MB 1963. I came on a Canadian Government Scholarship through Canadian International Development Agency (CIDA).

IF Was that a scholarship that meant you had to remain committed to Canada?

MB No. It is the sort of thing that meant; I should have gone back to Jamaica and worked for the Jamaican government for at least four years. I was bonded to the Jamaican government and returned in 1965, but returned to Canada in 1966.

IF What was the nature of your scholarship?

MB Teacher Training Industrial Education.

IF My idea of Industrial Education is more like welding/woodworking that sort of thing. Was that what you majored in?

MB Yes, technical trade technical and vocational. That is what I am qualified in.

IF Where in Jamaica are you from?

MB Ipswich, in St. Elizabeth.

IF	You said you have been volunteering for 38 years where did you learn your altruism?
MB	Basically right here in Toronto. There is a story behind that that I must tell. This is how I got involved in the Jamaican Canadian Association in 1964. I came to Canada in 1963 and I went to Saskatchewan and spent one school year there. I then moved to Toronto to attend the University of Toronto. I arrived in Toronto on a Wednesday evening, got off the train and went to check in at the YMCA at Bay and College (right where the Police Headquarters is today). After booking into the 'Y' I was told about the "WIF" Club the West Indies Federation Club at Brunswick and College. I went looking for the WIF club and made it to Spadina and College and I was picked up by a policeman for ***"fitting the description of a wanted Negro man."***
IF	You are not serious
MB	I am serious. I like telling this story because some people don't have a reason why they join the Association. I was picked up by a policeman for assaulted robbery and fitting the description of a man for assault and robbery. They took me to the Police Station. I did not have my identification on me (nothing on me). The sergeant allowed the police officer to take me back to the 'Y' for me to collect my ID which he did but he was not satisfied, so he took me back to the station with my papers. The sergeant looked at them and simply said, "Oh we are sorry, you are a victim of circumstances and you can go home. I said, go home where? I am in this city just about four hours ago and I was heading for a place where I was hoping to see some familiar faces. So all I need to do is to get there, so they took me there. That was when I met Harry Gairey who said to me, 'there is an association that was just formed a couple of years ago. You should not take it lying down; you should go and talk to the President. I know him. He is a young man, who just graduated from university. That is Roy Williams of course. So, I called them up and I was told that the Sunday was the General Meeting and I went and I gave my story from the floor and Roy said, 'we won't let that pass, we will write a letter on your behalf.' And they did. They wrote a letter to the Chief of Police, to the Province of Ontario—the Premier and to the Prime Minister, and all three sources responded and apologized to me. When I thought

	about what could have been, I figured that this Association has done something for me.
IF	What was Harry Gairey like?
MB	A little man with a big heart who has touched the lives of nearly every Jamaican and/or black person in the community. He was a part owner of WIF and it was the only club that West Indians could go to and everyone went there when they got a day off. He did his social work from the window where he served the meals at the club.
IF	What year was this?
MB	1964. And, I got involved as a member at that very meeting that Sunday and with the exception of the eight months that I spent back in Jamaica ('65/'66), I have been an active member of this Association continuously. I have held every position on this Board with the exception of Treasurer and Executive Secretary.
IF	The whole story has stunned me. I was going to ask you what was it like in Canada and how did you cope? I think you have answered much of those two questions, in the story you have told.
MB	A couple of books have been published and on the market that speaks to my existence in Canada. They don't have the story about the police, but my time in Canada "Discovering Patterns in Human Geography" and "Who's Who in Black Canada."
IF	So you became a member and have held almost all positions. What did you see the JCA's role as then and what do you see it as now?
MB	At that time I figured this class, white and subtle discriminatory society could be disastrous to quiet, easy-going people coming in. Based on the experience I had. As such, I saw JCA as an organization that could and would help people who found themselves in this sort of unfortunate situation. As I grew up with the JCA in Toronto, I see JCA as being able to help in directing people to the proper or right education to fit into this society. I see JCA as the organization that has done and still is directing newcomers in how to find places to live, counseling, type of education to go after and so on. I also see JCA as the organization that is going to provide the sort of advocacy that is necessary in most of the social endeavours education, health, housing because not everyone that arrives will know exactly what to do to get the best possible opportunities. I see JCA as the medium to assist people in these issues.

IF How would you say the JCA was operated and is that still the case?

MB The structure and format under which JCA has operated from the beginning until now, is very good. It is the sort of structure that prevents the JCA from becoming the personal commodity of an individual or a group of people. By virtue of having limitations and the democratic approach taken to select the leadership. I have seen other organizations that died natural deaths because of opposite structures.

IF What would you attribute JCA's general longevity to?

MB That's a good question and I would think there are a lot of reasons for it. JCA as an organization gets a lot of flack, a lot of criticism from people, but by the same token, most of the organizations that you see around Toronto, whatever they are, the people who originated those other organizations, got their ideas from the JCA or they have been at some point in time, a part of the JCA and they just want to be in something that they have ownership and leadership of so they go and form their own. So as a result, even though they have been in JCA and left, they still remember JCA out there. And as you know, advertising is that you sell yourself to someone to the point where he or she can't forget you and as long as you are on people's minds there is going to be some form of growth, just for being on peoples' minds. The second reason I think that JCA is such a formidable organization in this community, is, there has been a core group of membership, some of whom have died, but there is still a JCA core membership, who have stayed with the organization, they have stayed the course and even if they are not in leadership, positively or negatively, they impact the association, somehow.

IF Can you give me one or two successes that the JCA stood behind?

MB Job creation, in my mind is very important for the growth of a community and for the growth of people in general. Ever since this association got involved officially in social service programs and was funded somehow by government or other agencies, they have been in the business of job creation. In other words, there are many people in this city right now that I can put my hand on whose career or professions were started right here at JCA either on student employment when they were in high school or university or after school, whatever positions were available for which they qualified and after two or three years they moved on. JCA has really

	been a launching pad as no one can expect someone to spend a lifetime in JCA, but JCA has done a very good job of assisting.
IF	Would you say then, that many of the people that got launched here would not have had that opportunity in the wider sphere?
MB	Quiet honestly, no. And, especially those who have gone on and progressed in the social services field. They might not have had the opportunity to be exposed to that career, had JCA not been here. They would probably have had their first job in a store or some other area that would not have given them the opportunity to see this career path.
IF	What is the major difference you see, from your perspective, then and now with Jamaican and Canada?
MB	When I came to Toronto in 1964 of course anyone will tell you, you would walk long and hard to see another black person or another Jamaican so I guess the first observation that I can make is that, there is a 'helluva' lot more of us here between then and now. Because the numbers have grown, I think everything else has grown. I see more Jamaicans in this community acquiring decent jobs, things like houses, cars, more so now than they have in the past. But then, I can't help but noticing that the ills grow along with the good, so crime seems to be something that we are worried about among our young people. To be honest with you, for quite a long time, when there was a black crime, I used to take on some of the guilt, but these days, I have grown to recognize the fact that when you are a member of a community or you belong to an organization that you think has done its best to assist people socially, and if this sort of thing continues to happen, you don't blame yourself, you don't take on the guilt. You have done your best, and then you don't worry about what happens afterwards.
IF	On that point, I am sure you are aware that in the last week or so, the "mother country", if you will England, has imposed visa restrictions on Jamaicans going to England. What are your thoughts on that?
NB	My thoughts on that. Jamaica is an independent country and I remember before Jamaica became independent, England had no choice other than to accept anybody who bought a plane ticket, had a passport, jumped on a plane and got there. Jamaica became independent in 1962. We should be friendly to Britain, just as how we are to Canada or the United States. I think Britain reserves the right to put restrictions on any group of people that they think they

	want to. They do not owe Jamaica any obligations to give them any special privileges.
IF	What are your final thoughts particularly about JCA and your aspirations for JCA?
MB	I am involved in JCA from very close to the beginning. It was a long time coming from Dawes Road to Arrow Road, but it represents some form of growth. In other words, there is some measured growth between Dawes Road and Arrow Road. I remember a time when JCA used to employ 22 full-time staff plus summer staff. Over the past few years I have read about a lot of other groups that get tax payers money to do the things that this association has done for forty years and should be able to continue doing and in a greater way than in the past. I don't know how true this is, but I have heard that the staff is down to about 10 and I feel that something needs to be done to restore the numbers to what they use to be. Young people are coming and need to get the same opportunities that others got. I still look forward to the day when we can duplicate for this black community in Toronto something like the Columbus Centre at Dufferin and Lawrence.
IF	Thank You.
MB	Thank You.

JCA members bus it to Annual Picnic

Sub-Sectors, Activities, Affiliates and Sub-Groups

The JCA Membership

Membership in the Jamaican-Canadian Association consists of persons or groups who are, ... accepted as members . . . . and whose membership has not been terminated. There are four (4) categories of membership—Regular, Affiliate, Honorary and Lifetime. Regular Membership is open to all persons of Jamaican heritage and their families, and anyone else who shares the aims and objectives of the Association. Members are entitled to participate in all and every activity of the JCA. They may hold any office, for which they are qualified and to which they are elected. They may also serve on any committee of their choice. They are entitled to receive regular communication from the Association and they have the right to vote on issues presented at the Quarterly and Annual General Meetings. Lifetime Membership is usually conferred, following approval of the Board and the General Membership, on anyone who has made a significant contribution to the Association or community or who has been a member in good standing for at least twenty-five years. Lifetime Members are exempted from paying annual membership dues."[45] There currently are 22 lifetime members in the JCA.

Regular and Lifetime Members constitute the bulk of the membership in the Association. In the first year of the Association (1963) there were 237 regular members (See Appendix 5). Over the 50 years literally thousands have joined the Association. Thousands have also exited the Association over the same period. There is a high degree of transience where people join, stay a year or two or more, then they are never heard from or seen again. In some cases they have moved. The new address and phone number is never communicated to the JCA. Hundreds of letters are returned to the JCA or are simply dumped by the current occupant at the given address. Some will have left due to age or lack of, or loss of interest in what was or is happening at the JCA. Some will have left because their new residence is remote from the JCA—Brampton, Mississauga, Markham, Pickering, Whitby or elsewhere and they may have joined other organizations that have been established in their neighbourhoods. Whatever the reason the JCA membership fluctuates constantly, rising during periods of intense activity triggered by a crisis, disaster or public profile and receding thereafter to peak again after an appropriate interval.

Fluctuating Membership

Despite that history of volatility there is a hard core of loyal members who have supported the Association continuously for 10, 15, 20, 30, 40 years and there are currently about 10 members who have supported the Association from the year of its founding to the present day—50 years. This is the core of the JCA—the bulk of whom are female. This longevity of membership is also reflected in the increasing average age of the membership which is now about 55 years of age.

There is the perception held by the public that the JCA is a large and powerful organization with thousands of members. This perception likely is the result of the JCA's loud voice as it relentlessly advocates on behalf of the disadvantaged, voiceless and underrepresented people of all stripes over the years, and as it battles inequality and injustice in the system. Although it barks very loudly, in reality its membership fluctuates over time anywhere from less than one hundred (100) to a little less than five hundred (500) with the mean being around 250.

The Membership Chairperson hardly ever reports the total membership in any given year and it is assumed that the total membership consists of those who have paid their membership dues plus those members who are in arrears, which would number into several hundreds. On occasion there is exultation over the number of new members gained as the chairperson did in her 1981 report "our membership list has swelled by the total of 88 new members."[46] Herman Stewart as Membership Chairperson in 1994 reported that they recruited 51, 79 and 54 new members in 1992, 1993 and part of 1994 but they had lost 75 of these due to non renewals. This highlights the very high membership attrition rate.

Mr. Stewart, during the time that he was president (1996-2001), set a target of adding at least 150 new members each year. The Annual Reports for 1997, 1998 and 1999 reported 160, 170, and 235 new members respectively and in his final report to the membership in 2001 stated "We also increased our membership by over 600 new members."[47]

The Membership Chairperson in 2009 reported "465 active members and 600 inactive/dormant members."[48] and in 2011 "We now have 333 paid up members; our goal is 500 members by the end of the next fiscal year."[49] The fluctuation and the transience continues; however, the year 2012 should be a good year for membership growth as there will be many events celebrating the 50th anniversary of the founding of the Association and the independence of Jamaica.

Large Jamaican Population

Immigration data reveals that 100,300 Jamaican immigrants selected Ontario as their destination province between the years 1973 to 1996. That number represents 86 percent of total Jamaican Immigration to Canada in that period. Fifty-four percent were female vs. 46 percent male. (See Tables 2 in Appendix 2). Data from the 2001 Census reveals that Ontario was the home to eighty-five per cent (85%) of the total Canadian population with Jamaican ethnic roots, and that year there were 181,000 people with Jamaican origins living in Ontario.[50] Not only do most live in Ontario, ninety per cent (90%) of these live in large urban centres—Toronto, Brampton, Mississauga, Hamilton and surrounding Greater Toronto Areas (GTA).

Deterrence to Membership

Why then is membership in the JCA not larger than it is? Some theories advanced are: (1) Jamaicans are individualistic and are ill inclined to join organizations; (2) when they do join they tend to join groups to which they have previously established bonds, e.g. alumni associations (Old Boys, Old Girls networks, churches) and there is an abundance of these; (3) Jamaicans are snobs and are therefore very selective of the groups to which they choose to belong; (4) Jamaicans are very class conscious and may rate a group as below their social class; (5) there are ethnic divisions within the Jamaican community which presents a barrier to some; (6) many have never heard of the JCA; (7) many (including doctors, dentists, lawyers, accountants, business persons) are too busy with work, their profession, family and other commitments; and (8) some may not see the JCA as the vehicle that is likely to satisfy their social, psychic and self-actualization needs. Going forward into its next 50 years of existence the JCA, therefore, will need to develop a strategy to attract a larger core membership and to retain its new recruits, especially young members, as the average age of the current membership is about 55.

The most loyal members are those who came in the early years—the 1960's, 1970's and the early 1980's when they needed to stand together and fight issues together. They needed the comfort and support of their association. They also were emotionally, physically and psychically invested in actually building the association. They rolled up their sleeves and got their hands dirtied. More recent recruits are viewing the finished product and are able to enjoy the significantly altered lifestyle conditions resulting from the earlier struggles. They may not think that there is much that they can contribute to the Association.

Cost of Membership

The cost to individuals to join and maintain membership in the JCA has been very modest and has not likely been a deterrent. From 1962 until about 1968 the annual fee was Two Dollars ($2.00); then it was increased to Three Dollars ($3.00). In 1972 the fee was increased to Five Dollars ($5.00) and to Ten Dollars ($10.00) in 1982. In 1998 the fee was increased to Twenty Dollars ($20.00) per year single and Thirty Dollars ($30.00) per family. The current annual membership fee is $25.00 per person, $35.00 per family and $10.00 for seniors. This is still quite modest, quite reasonable and quite affordable to most people.

Communicating With Members

A critical ingredient of member adhesion is information about the Association and its current and future activities. Members need to feel a part of what is happening and to be always in the know. At the inception of the Association the communication mode was primarily person to person, word of mouth, telephone and a monthly Newsletter.

The Newsletter was written by the president, typed by the recording secretary on a stencil and then reproduced on the aforementioned Mimeograph duplicator. The remaining tasks involved addressing envelopes, folding and inserting the newsletter, sealing, affixing postage to the envelopes and depositing them at the mail box. These latter tasks would be performed collectively. A date would be identified for the production of the Newsletter and the Executive would assemble to perform these tasks. Many hands made the work go fast, so that it hardly seemed like work. It was another occasion to interact with each other, to get to know each other, to make friends with each other. It was social bonding. Extra copies of the newsletter would be deposited at barber shops, beauty salons and West Indian grocery stores. So too were flyers for dances and other special events.

As time went on and a membership committee was formed the task of overseeing the production and distribution of the Newsletter was delegated to that committee. The president contributed and each committee was responsible for producing information on recent occurrences and upcoming events. Articles were contributed by others from time to time. The Newsletter was either produced in-house when we had duplicating equipment or was produced at some members' workplace on borrowed equipment. The ritual of collectively gathering to fold, insert, label and stamp the envelopes was retained. Again it was a social, team-building event.

Over the years as the membership grew they began to disperse quite widely across the Greater Toronto Area. Getting together became more difficult. The cost of paper, envelopes and stamps escalated and the JCA's finances were lean. As a consequence the number and frequency of Newsletters declined. The original intention of a monthly newsletter was now out of the question. It became a bi-monthly publication, followed later by a quarterly publication. Even this was not always met. The Newsletter became sporadic. Lack of information resulted in lack of interest and coincided with consequent apathy and decline in membership.

A New Era in Communications

With the resurgence of the Jamaican-Canadian Association in the 1980's there was also a resurgence in its communications internally and externally. On April 24, 1985 with the assistance of Ryerson Journalism intern Donna Yawching the JCA launched the first edition of its new publication in tabloid newspaper format. A new mast head and logo was designed and *InFocus* the new JCA print media came into existence. Several issues of *InFocus* were published in this format but it was costly and the in-house journalistic resources were not always available.

Fortunately by this time in the 1980's the JCA had begun to acquire computers and the staff and some committee members had began to become computer literate. Before long their word processing skills had progressed to the point that the *InFocus* could be produced internally. Over the years since then with the availability of Desktop Publishing software and staff and member improved computing skills the *In Focus* continued to be published mostly quarterly. Over the years also the masthead and logo have gone through many transformations. Recently the *In Focus* has appeared in photo magazine format, is being printed externally, is no longer being mailed to members and is available only at membership meetings to those who attend. Its content has also varied in terms of quality, substance and importance to the community and the association's members. In the past there have been excellent articles on the ethnic and racial composition of the Jamaican population, on Marcus Garvey; on Violence in the Black Community and other issues of substance that should be continued. The *In Focus* has the potential to be an excellent means of championing and espousing the issues that the JCA cares about to edify and advocate for the community. Its message content and reach can be improved.

Electronic Media

In addition to the print media the JCA also uses the internet to communicate. Its first website was developed in the late 1990's and for years it was quite inert. Information on the site was often out of date. However, in recent times the website *www.jcaontario.org* has been redesigned and it is more informative. It tells about JCA, its founding, its social service programs, recent activities and upcoming events. It is a vast improvement from earlier times and it is still capable of further development.

With the widespread availability of computers and the internet the JCA has also utilized email to communicate with members. From time to time there is an email blast where urgent matters or reminders are sent out to those who are on the email list. Although both the website and the email are modern means of communicating with a mass audience much of that audience is not up to date on the technology. It is unlikely that a majority of the members have computers, access the internet and use email. There is a generation gap that hopefully will be dispelled in future. There is also an attempt to use U-tube, facebook, twitter and other social media but they too face an even greater generation technology deficit. Thus there is a return, quite often, to the use of the labour-intensive, less-effective telephone blitz.

Image Make-Over

In 1987, with a grant from the Secretary of State, Multiculturalism, the JCA published its 25-year Anniversary booklet "Jamaicans in Canada, a Commitment to Excellence." In this booklet Jamaicans living in every province in Canada were memorialized for their ongoing contributions and accomplishments in their adopted country. As a by-product of this venture we had the opportunity to redesign the JCA logo and thus was born the black, green and gold triple-crowned emblem that now adorns the letterheads, envelopes and all other JCA communications and documents.

The JCA Logo

Roy Williams presents Mayor Eggleton a copy of "Jamaicans in Canada"

The Jamaican-Canadian Association Community Centre

Does the Jamaican Canadian Community really need its own building? What is the relevance of the building to the existence of the association? When one looks around one notices that the Jews have their synagogues. The Moslems have their mosques. The Sikhs and the Hindus have their magnificent temples. The Christians have their cathedrals. The Chinese have their cultural centers. The Japanese have their cultural center. All of these are testaments about the people. They testify to the existence of the sect in Canada. They testify to their identity. They testify to their transition from transience to permanence. They testify to the movement from individualistic impotence to the potential of collective potency. They testify to the act of coalescing. They testify to the emergence of a collective voice.

The physical structure of a building—The Jamaican-Canadian Centre—in itself transforms the Association from an intangible entity, in the minds of many, to a tangible reality. It is something that one can actually see. It is a place that one can go to. It is a place where people gather. It is a place where activities take place. It is a place where one can become physically involved and make a contribution according to one's ability. It is symbolic.

In 1988 when Hurricane Gilbert devastated Jamaica the JCA Centre served as the Command and Control Center for the hurricane relief effort. It is the place where community activists met and founded the Black Action Defense Committee (BADC) in 1988. It is the place where the community honored Donovan Bailey upon his becoming the 1996 Olympic 100 meter champion. It is the place where in 2009 the community welcomed Usain Bolt, the 2008 Olympic 100 meter champion and world's fastest man. It is the place where the Haiti Earthquake Relief fundraiser was held in 2010 and was quickly followed by the Fundraiser for the flood victims of Tropical Storm Nicole in Jamaica. It is the place where the community gathered to honour celebrated activist Dudley Laws and to have his Wake prior to his funeral.

It is the place where the community gathered to have a Town Hall meeting with Police Chief Bill Blair in 2010 and it is the place where the community honoured Deputy Chief Peter Sloley and Deputy Chief Keith Forde. It is the place where the Community Mayors' All-Candidates meeting was held before the 2010 Toronto municipal election. It is the place where the Prime Minister of Jamaica and other Jamaica government ministers meet with Jamaicans on their periodic visits to Toronto. It is the place where the Jamaica Diaspora Foundation meets from time to time. It is the place where many Alumni Associations and other community groups celebrate their annual or other periodic events

It is the place where the Caribbean Canadian Seniors meet twice weekly to reminisce and to rejuvenate. It is the place where many senior men gather weekly to play domino. It is the place where the Health Fair is held, annually. It is the place where the Mothers' Day Brunch, the Seniors' Dinner and the Children's Christmas Party are held. It is the place where the Boononoooonus Brunch is held and where the Black History Month celebration for the children is held. It is the place where the Annual Scholarship Dinner and Awards is held. It is the place where the Saturday Morning Tutorial Program, to help struggling students, is held. It is a place where concerts and theatrical productions are sometimes presented. It is a place where wedding receptions, birthdays and other significant events are celebrated by both JCA members and non members.

It is also the place where programs, services and counselling is offered to disaffected children and youth, families in turmoil, distressed and abused women and where employment services and counselling is provided for the unemployed and underemployed.

The JCA truly functions as a community centre and that is the reason that it fought so long and so hard over the years to acquire its own building. It is a testament that we can own something of value that testifies to our presence and our permanence. It is the place where visiting dignitaries from Jamaica are sometimes hosted by the Consul General.

Toronto 2010 Mayoral Candidates—George Smitherman, Rocco Achampong and Joe Pantalone

Attendees lined up to question 2010 Mayoral Candidate at the JCA Centre

Financing the JCA Over the Years

The JCA from its founding in 1962 has been a self-financing organization. It obtains its revenues primarily from membership dues and fundraising events. Fundraising events typically include dances, raffles, bus trips, walkathons, bazaars, bake sales bingo and recently a golf tournament. In addition there are the standard annual events such as the Independence Dinner and Dance, the New Year's Eve Party, the summer picnic, the Bononoonous Brunch, Mother's Day and Seniors' Brunches which are not primarily fundraising events but which, from time to time, may turn a small profit. In addition the JCA, on occasion, gets donations from some of its members. The success and profitability of all the above are positively correlated with the quality and intensity of the marketing effort and the members' co-operation and full participation in the events.

In the latter years there has been an additional source of income through interest earned as a result of short-term investments of cash which results from the receipt of funds in advance of the performance of the contracted services for government or other funders. There is also the rental from the banquet halls once the JCA acquired a building. Special fundraising campaigns were launched for special projects like the Building Fund, where substantial amount of money was being sought. The JCA would ask for and receive large donations and pledges of future contributions. Donations in small as well as large amounts would be welcomed. There were "Buy-A-Brick" appeals as well as naming opportunities for a door, a window, a room, or other aspects of the building that were associated with more substantial donations. There was also the opportunity to purchase a bond for five (5) years at attractive interest rates. All of the above have been used over the years with remarkable success.

All of the JCA activities involving its advocacy and interventions up until 1979 were without receipt of a single dime from any level of government. In 1979 there was the grand sum of $8,738 recorded by the treasurer as government grants (no further explanation). With this amount included the JCA had gross revenues of $23,219. When the $16,452 of expenses were deducted there was an excess of revenue over expenditures of $6,767. Without the government grant expenses would have exceeded the income of $14,352 resulting in a net loss of $2,100. This shows just how close to the margin the JCA had been operating.

Financial information prior to 1979 is unavailable. One can only imagine the dire situation experienced by the JCA in that earlier period. With the small inflow of limited government funding the JCA's cash position became somewhat more stable, still it experienced a net increase of expenditures over income (net loss) of $2.678 and $1,494 in 1981 and 1982 respectively.[51]

As the JCA was able to make a case for obtaining government funding beginning in the early part of the 1980's and after becoming a United Way agency in 1988, more stable funding began to flow to the JCA. Because the funding agencies sometimes paid up front for the contracted services to be rendered the JCA was able to place the money in short term investments thereby earning interest as an added source of income. A review of the Table on JCA finances (Table 3 Appendix 9) and the Table on JCA Funds Flow from external funders, (Table 4 below) shows the marked progression in JCA's financial position over successive 10-year periods and similarly the external funding received over the similar periods beginning with 1979.

JCA has been fortunate to have attracted a succession of treasurers over the years who were scrupulously honest and most meticulous in paying attention to every detail relating to the inflow of funds, the proper security of those funds, the careful disbursement thereof, and the regular reporting to the members at quarterly and Annual General Meetings. This required hundreds of volunteer hours, especially as the accounting became more complex with the multiplicity of funders and the contingent reporting requirements. Thanks to Frank Wallace, Cyndi Anderson and all the other treasurers; and a special Thank You to Mrs. Sheila Simpson, CA, the JCA's first Chartered Accountant external auditor who spent countless unpaid hours organizing and arranging things in the proper order and also training some of the treasurers.

Table 4

TOTAL FUNDS RECEIVED FROM EXTERNAL FUNDERS
10-Year Periods—1972 Through to 2011

Year	Amt.	Year	Amt.	Year	Amt.	Year	Amt.
1972	0	1982	160820	1992	656249	2002	668221
1973	0	2983	214565	1993	1221825	2003	675881
1974	6000	1984	166686	1994	N/A	2004	752850
1975	7100	1985	11200	1995	1086303	2005	780419
1976	15400	1986	114991	1996	1084303	2006	935288
1977	0	1987	136183	1997	536345	2007	1451486
1978	0	1988	114241	1998	1058888	2008	1606619
1979	8738	1989	445233	1999	566165	2009	1649611
1980	12383	1990	358302	2000	637846	2010	1656415
1981	10128	1991	374454	2001	587949	2011	1618887
TOTAL	59749	TOTAL	2096675	TOTAL	7435873	TOTAL	11795677

Total over the period 1972 to 2011—$21,387,974.

Source—JCA Annual Financial Statements.
Year 1994 was unavailable.

JCA "Stalwarts at Work"

Social and Community Service

After the immigration door opened in the late 1950's, 1960's and beyond Jamaicans poured into Canada in large numbers. Immigration statistics reveal that 62,733 Jamaicans immigrated to Canada between 1973 and 1984 and 53000 of them settled in Ontario. Between 1985 and 1996 a further 53,666 Jamaicans arrived and 47300 of them settled in Ontario. The total number of Jamaicans immigrating to Canada in the period 1973 to 1996 was 116,399 and of that number 100,300 chose to settle in Ontario leaving the remaining 16,099 to be distributed among the remaining nine provinces and territories.

While a few of these Jamaicans would end up in rural Ontario it is widely known that they are urban dwellers. The majority of them would choose to live in urban centres like the City of Toronto and the Greater Toronto Area. It does not require a great stretch of the imagination to realize that there would be an enormous demand for services to facilitate the settlement and adaptation process. Finding a suitable place to live at a reasonable cost is a first essential. Finding a suitable job is of equal importance. Getting to know where everything is and where needed services may be obtained is essential. Getting to know the city and its transportation system is important. Getting to understand the culture, idioms and appropriate modes of conduct and communication is vital. They would need to deal with all of this and more in an environment that was not always the most welcoming and friendly.

While all of the above are challenging to the adults, consider the situation for children and teen-agers who have an even greater adjustment to make to a school system that is alien to them, where they are now in the minority, and with teachers who oft times consider them to be less able. They may live in a single-parent, female-headed household and may be reuniting after several years of separation from a parent they barely know. Also there are two-parent families where both parents have full-time jobs, or the single parent has two jobs. In both cases the parents have little time for the children and teenagers. They may live in low-income, assisted or social housing with few amenities. It is well documented that the earnings of visible minorities and women are several percentage points lower than that of whites and males and that they are more likely to be employed in low-level factory jobs and in service jobs and they experience higher rates of unemployment than whites. This would dictate a lower standard and level of living. They may not be able to provide their children and teenagers with their desired lifestyle and the apparel and paraphernalia enjoyed by their peers or reference group.

To whom do these new immigrants with needs turn for help? Quite often it is to the only well established Caribbean/black organization—The Jamaican-Canadian Association (JCA). The settlement and adaptation problems encountered by rapid, mass immigration if not anticipated and provided for often result in social disorientation and social disorder. It is not surprising that antisocial and deviant behaviours developed in certain segments of the city and those neighbourhoods began to be stigmatized.

The Jamaican-Canadian Association which had not been established as a primary social service delivery agency suddenly found itself having to respond to the needs of a sizeable and growing segment of the population which included other immigrant groups as well. This was done by volunteers without government financial support. The first "official" organized step in providing service started in 1975 with the acquisition of or (merging with) an Immigrant Counselling Service called the Activities and Information Centre that was located at 913 Bathurst Street. The service was fully funded from a Manpower Immigrant Settlement purchase of service contract in 1976 with application submitted for renewal for 1977-1978. With this amalgamation came two full-time staff that provided job counselling and placement, referrals for housing, family counselling and immigration services. Funds obtained from government in 1975 and 1976 were $7100 and $15,400 respectively.[52]

The JCA was already active in the education area in four junior high schools in North York where the Caribbean Outreach Program and the Booster program were being introduced. In 1980 grants were received from the Ontario and federal governments for two (2) Youth Summer Programs which employed three (3) workers, and the Primary Preventative Program in the Jane-Finch area; the co-ordinator and a staff of two. The association was also able to hire an Office Co-ordinator. Strangely the treasurer's report shows only $12,382 as Government grants in 1980. By 1982 for similar activities the government funding is reported at $160,829. Governments continued to support the Caribbean Outreach Project; the Preventative Program in the targeted areas (Jane-Finch, Lawrence Heights and Threthewey) on a short-term project-oriented basis. The United Way made its first contribution of $5000 to the JCA in 1984 and the total external funding support from all sources in 1984 was $166,686.

An Emerging Social Service Agency (CYFS)

The funding for the Caribbean Outreach Program, which was started about 1980, during the regimes of Mel Thompson and Rupert James, was discontinued in July, 1984. It was replaced by the Caribbean Youth Program which was intended to serve young persons ranging in age from 12 to 24 years and was funded by the Ministry of Social and Community Services. This funding was much more stable than the temporary project funding of the Preventative Program and the Outreach Program. In April 1988 the JCA became a full fledged United Way agency. The Caribbean Youth Program had become the Caribbean Youth and Family Services (CYFS) a full fledged social service delivery agency operating out of offices at 2065 Finch Avenue West and serving clients of every description in the Jane-Finch and the greater northwest Toronto area. There was another office in the Lawrence Heights area manned by Akwatu Khenti and Chris Spence (now Dr. Chris Spence). There also was the JCA head office at 1621 Dupont Street in Toronto. The paid staff had now increased to nine persons; however the external funding from all sources was still a paltry $114,241.

The CYFS had now emerged as an agency sponsored by the JCA, or an affiliate of the JCA, or a subsidiary of the JCA, or a branch of the JCA or an integral part of the JCA. This is a situation that still needs clarification. In 1998 the CYFS moved from its former location at 2065 Finch Avenue West to its new headquarters at 995 Arrow Road.

Other Service Entities

In addition to the Caribbean Youth and Family Services JCA also offers the **Caribbean Immigrant Services** with the purpose of assisting immigrants in settling and adapting to life in Canada. This was the Immigrant Settlement and Adaptation Program (ISAP) which was funded by Employment and Immigration Canada. This program was started in 1986 with Everton Cummings as its first Co-ordinator and continued until 2005 when the government terminated the funding. There also was the **Multicultural and Community Services** component which involves the interaction with other agencies, groups and individuals to enable them to better understand our culture and to enable them to better interact with this ethno cultural group. This took us to every segment of society, viz. schools, churches, courts, governments, and other organizations. It involves giving speeches, conducting fora, workshops, conferences, networking, public appearances and public relations efforts.

Fast Forward to 2011-2012

During the more than two decades since 1988 the demand for social and community services have continued to increase at an exponential rate. This required a response both in quantity, quality and range of services offered. The social and community services arm of the Jamaican-Canadian Association is now housed in the JCA Centre at 995 Arrow Road. It has a staff of 20 (a CEO, Program Manager, Accountant, 4 Program Co-ordinators, Receptionist and 12 Social Worker-Counsellors). The service has four main components:

- Caribbean Youth and Family Services
- Caribbean Immigrant Services
- Employment Ontario
- Multicultural/Intercultural and Community services

There are 5 components to the **Caribbean Youth and Family Services**:

1—Leaders in Partnership Program (L.I.P.) serves the needs of young children 7-12 in the school system to achieve normative behaviour standards.
2—K-Club (Transition Program) provides group and individual counselling to young persons aged 16-24 to effect their rehabilitation to positive social behaviours.
3—Youth Outreach Worker—serves to engage youths age 12-21 and their families and connect them with available services.
4—Parenting Program—provides individual support, family mediation, counselling to individuals and families.
5—Violence Against Women (VAW)—provides support to women and children who are experiencing or have experienced domestic violence.

The **Caribbean Immigrant Services** has two (2) components:

1—Newcomer Settlement Program—assists newcomers residing in Canada by providing support and information on various matters (employment, housing, etc.)
2—Settlement and Adaptation Program—serves newcomers who have been in the Country three (3) years or less (counselling, referrals, sponsorship, etc.).

The **Employment Ontario**—deals with assisting clients to become gainfully employed (Job Search, Job Training, Resource and Information, Job Matching, Referral).

The **Multicultural/Intercultural and Community Services**—involves interacting with other Groups, agencies, entities and systems to better understand them and their cultures and to enable them to better understand the Caribbean/black ethno cultural group, its languages, behaviours, mores, idioms, religions, symbols, and culture. This may include issues of race, ethnicity, equity, equality, social justice, equal treatment, affirmative action, and reasonable accommodation. (This aspect is a responsibility of senior management but should also be interwoven in all the programs and carried out by all program personnel. This is not currently being practiced.)

Summer Day Camp—From time to time the JCA has sought funding to operate a Summer Day Camp which furnishes summer employment for college and university students and provides needed recreational and other learning experiences for young children.

Summary

The Social and Community Services of the JCA has made tremendous strides over the years as it moved from a purely volunteer, unfunded service to its constituents to its situation today as a United Way agency that receives funding from different levels of government, foundations and the United Way. Has it been a smooth transition? Has it been as successful as it could have been? The answer to both questions is negative. The major warts here have been instability due to an inability to retain competent staff and management. There has been close to a dozen Executive Directors over the period some of whom have stayed less than 12 months. Competent staff have left for better paying positions or positions that offered upward mobility opportunities and/or professional growth. Critical reporting deadlines have been missed from time to time which has resulted in problems with the funders, and the agency has been downgraded on occasion following periodic evaluations. In addition because its board is also the Board of Directors for the JCA there is frequent turnover of volunteer board members as the JCA constitution mandates term limits on its board members. New incoming members to the board quite often are inexperienced and have no knowledge of social and community service issues. As a consequence the Social Services delivery area may not have received the quality of leadership that it deserves if it had its own Board, independent of the JCA internal issues. This needs to be remedied—soon.

Despite the warts mentioned above taken on its overall merits the JCA has to be complimented for bringing this agency into existence and taking it to this level as only one of two agencies that serves the Caribbean/black community and the first to do so starting from its volunteer days. Growing pains are not unusual for volunteer organizations. To have survived for 50 years is an exceptional accomplishment and it is to be highly commended. Progress, development and growth results as one learns from past experiences and one takes the necessary corrective steps.

JCA Staff Members

JCA Women at play

JCA Walkathon women

Innovative Fundraising—
The JCA Walkathon

The Jamaican-Canadian Association had acquired its first building "JAMAICA HOUSE" in 1971. That satisfied an aspiration that existed since its founding in 1962. Unfortunately within a year that building burned to the ground. That was a devastating loss that shook the members to the core. They, however, vowed by hook or crook to replace the building. From the proceeds of the sale of the land they purchased land on Danforth Avenue in east end Toronto to become the site of the future "JAMAICA HOUSE." The members greatly desired to have their own place.

There was too much wandering around during the years following the 1972 fire loss. There was further devastation when the land for the future building had to be sold in 1978 because there was no money flowing in with which to build the desired structure. Yet the members remained resolute. The indomitable Mr. Alton Telfer, for various periods of time over the years, undertook to chair the Building Committee and later on the Fundraising Committee. He tried different tactics to raise funds. These included fundraising dances at various rented halls where he would net approximately $1,000.00 per event. He would hold Bazaars and Bake Sales which would net approximately $500.00. There were small raffles from time to time. There was always a constant searching for innovative ways to raise funds.

In 1982 the light dawned. In a telephone conversation between Daphne Bailey, the chair of the Membership Committee, and the late Juanita Thompson, committee member and fervent JCA member, the idea of a walkathon was broached. Did Juanita come up with the idea or was it Daphne? Whichever of the two suggested it, that is where the idea of the walkathon was born, and either one or both can take credit for it. Daphne, of course, as chair of the committee acted upon the idea and immediately set about to organize the first JCA walkathon.

A walkathon involves many people each walking (jogging or running) along a designated route consisting of either five (5) kilometres or 10 kilometres. Each walker receives a lump sum donation from several supporters for completing the designated route or a certain amount of money per each kilometre completed. It is important to get many walkers, each having many supporters and each supporter contributing many dollars in order to maximize the walkathon outcome. There is little or no financial expense. All that is required is physical effort.

The March to City Hall

On a rainy Saturday morning in May, 1982 the first walkathon was held. Despite the inclement weather 10 hardy souls turned out. Zenover Brown, Hermine Johnson, Barry Johnson, Juanita Thompson, Roy B. Stewart, Raphael Walters, Lorna Plummer, Alton Telfer, Bernice Bailey and Daphne Bailey were the very first walkers. They walked from the then offices of the JCA, 2400 Dufferin Street, all the way down to Toronto City Hall. President Rupert James provided a motorized escort and dispensed steaming hot coffee to the walkers, as needed, along the way. After completing the walk the walkers dispersed or went back to the office to retrieve their belongings. There was a feeling of elation and satisfaction. They had initiated a new fundraising vehicle, one in which everyone could participate. There was a spirit of camaraderie among the band of walkers. They had raised $2,600.00 for the JCA. In 1982 that was a significant accomplishment for a one-off event with no expenses to deduct.

Institutionalization

The walkathon, the first Saturday or Sunday in May became a tradition at the JCA and a scheduled event on its fundraising calendar. In addition people began to see the health benefits of a brisk walk on an early Spring morning after a long winter hibernation. It was also a social occasion as it provided the opportunity for many people to meet and greet each other after the long winter isolation.

Over the years the early band of 10 walkers began to grow to become many walkers. Some came from the east in Metro Toronto and others came from the west. This called for management and organization. The city was divided into east and west and an eastern and a western team was created. A team captain was appointed for each team. This naturally resulted in competition as to which team could raise the most money each year. There was also the individual competition as to which individual would raise the most money each year. There were the perennial winners: Kamala-Jean Gopie, Bruce McDonald, Daphne Bailey, Fay and Vincent Conville and the late Juanita Thompson. This was joyful competition and the competitors felt good about their successes. After a while trophies began to be awarded to the winners.

The time spanning the years 1980's, 1990's and early 2000's the walkathon effort was championed from time to time by the then current Fundraising Committee chairperson: Daphne Bailey, Vincent Pusey, Bruce McDonald or Fay/Vincent Conville. They raised large sums of money: 1991—$6,643, 1993—5,187, 1990—$10,000, 1996—$15,554 and 2000—$11,074.

In 2010 the planning for the walkathon took on a more professional approach. That required a higher level of organization. Ms Sandra Whiting consented to head the JCA Walkathon Ad-Hoc Committee. She was ably assisted by the JCA Women's Committee and the regular Walkathon organizers. "Walk Good" (borrowed from the legendary Miss Lou) became the slogan. This group worked day and night to bring about a spectacular 2010 "Walk Good" Walkathon result. It became not solely a JCA event. It became a community walkathon. Six community groups participated. Twelve patrons signed on and $30,000 was raised. This became the base upon which to build. As a result in 2011 there were 13 participating community organizations. There were approximately 300 walkers and they raised $45,000. First, second and third prizes were awarded in different categories for monies raised and/or for completing the 5K and 10K routes.

The little idea that evolved during the telephone conversation in 1982 has grown to become a significant event in the black/ Caribbean community. It is a social happening. It is an inter-community event. It is a physical fitness activity and it is a community fundraising event. In 2012 the walkathon will be celebrating its 30th year. It should be another banner year.

JCA Walkathon participants warming up for walk

Boonoonoonos Brunch At JCA: The Beginning

By Erma Collins, B.A., M.Ed.

Background

Like golf at JCA, the Boonoonoonos Brunch grew out of the Capital Fundraising Committee of the late 1990's to the early 2000's, an ad hoc committee established by the Board, under the leadership of Herman Stewart. JCA having only recently acquired 995 Arrow Road, the committee's mandate was to go beyond JCA members, to corporations and other individuals, to raise moneys towards our "Building to Serve" funds. In 1999, the second year of the committee's existence, the members were Erma Collins (Chair), Paul Barnett, Vincent Conville, Dr. Buddy McIntosh, Dr. Ezra Nesbeth, Lana Salmon-Jones, Herman Stewart (JCA's President), Sandra Whiting, and Patricia Williams (JCA's Fundraising Committee Chair).

Brainstorming

During the United Way's blackout period from September to December, when its agencies are prohibited from approaching corporations, the committee came up with many fundraising ideas. Among them was one for a Celebrity Brunch, to take place during Black History Month the next February. We defined "celebrity" as those among us who had excelled in different fields like medicine, law, engineering, media, finance, education, entrepreneurship, politics, technology, arts & entertainment, sports, hospitality, labour, human resource management, and so on. As the group developed its ideas for the brunch, Sandra Whiting suggested that we give it a catchy name. She came up with "boonoonoonos"; it clicked with the rest of us.

We decided to have a celebrity at every table. There would be minimal if any entertainment. We wanted people to interact with the celebrity and with one another. There would be Black History quizzes; people would be asked to make up limericks, to sing songs, to have fun—all facilitated by the celebrity.

Sunday, February 20, 2000

The inaugural Boonoonoonos Brunch and Brawta, on February 20, 2000, was a knockout affair. All of 47 celebrity hosts turned up and were introduced and seated with pomp and ceremony. Guests were welcomed by our patron, the Hon. Lincoln Alexander. Jamaican Consul General Herman LaMont brought greetings. Judge Stanley Grizzle said grace. Caterer Jean McIntosh treated us to a sumptuous meal. There was a piano rendition by Melanie Anne Atkins and a skit by Jones and Jones. Then the fun began.

MC Sandra Whiting did an excellent job getting celebrities to lead their tables in singing songs from assigned themes; to answer items from the quiz (prepared by Vincent Conville); to expand one or two given lines into a limerick (prepared by Erma Collins); and to pay whatever amount of money she decided, whenever she decided that the job was not up to par or was too well done. People left with wide grins on their faces and with the request that JCA "do it again next year."

The Caribbean Camera reported that "the fun-filled event was a huge success." *Share* reported that "the community turned out in full force" and that "MC Sandra Whiting did an amazing job of keeping the afternoon activities hot, hot, hot." Committee Chair Erma Collins was happy to report to the JCA Board that the event had netted $11,052, with the help of sponsors (Judge Pamela Appelt, Paul Barnett and Associates, Don's Meat and West Indian Restaurant, Lawyer Aston Hall, Jamaica National, Dr. Ezra Nesbeth, Ontario Federation of Labour, and Lana Salmon-Jones).

Afterwards

In February 2001, the committee (Paul Barnett [Chair], Victor Anderson, Erma Collins, Vincent Conville, Dr. Ezra Nesbeth, Barbara Thomas, Herman Stewart [JCA's President], and Sandra Whiting) repeated the format. Hon. Lincoln Alexander and the late Mrs Beverly Mascoll were patrons. A celebrity that year, Raynier Maharaj of *The Caribbean Camera,* wrote: "If you missed the fundraising Boonoonoonos Brunch and Brawta, you missed out. It was a grand time, with celebrities at every table where, betwixt and between nibbling on delicacies like curried goat and green fig, we had to get the folks to do something outrageous . . . . The real star was *Pride's* Van Cooten, who got up on the stage to render us all speechless with a beautiful song."

Nothing remains static. The event has taken on different permutations since its inauguration in 2000. The Capital Fundraising Committee was wrapped up but Boonoonoonos Brunch at the JCA has remained a staple during Black History Month each year. It has been produced by the regular Fundraising Committee, by Jones and Jones, as well as by Sandra Whiting and Associates. It has morphed from an interactive event to an entertainment-based one. But it has endured.

Participants at a JCA event

Golf At The Jamaican Canadian Association (JCA)

A BRIEF HISTORY (Contributed by Erma Collins, B.A., M.Ed.)

Introduction and Background

It is said that no man is an island, that we are all interconnected; that one small event can mushroom into something unimagined; that small streams can merge to form mighty rivers. Golf at JCA has been something like that.

In 1998, the visionary Herman Stewart, then president of the JCA, asked Bromley Armstrong, Erma Collins, and Kamala-Jean Gopie to spearhead a Capital Fundraising Committee (CFC). The purpose was to outreach to corporations and individuals in the non-Jamaican communities, to help raise funds for our newly-acquired Jamaican-Canadian Centre on Arrow Road. In April of 1999, Kamala-Jean had to withdraw from the committee to take up a government appointment, and she relinquished the chairmanship to Erma. The reconstituted committee (Paul Barnett, Erma Collins, Vincent Conville, Dr. Buddy McIntosh, Dr. Ezra Nesbeth, Lana Salmon-Jones, Herman Stewart, Sandra Whiting, and Pat Williams) left no stone unturned.

One element that had to be factored into the group's planning was that the JCA, as a United Way Agency, was not allowed to approach corporations during the United Way Campaign from September to December each year. Therefore, as September of '99 approached, the CFC brainstormed ideas for raising funds during the blackout period. Pat Williams, who was also chair of JCA's regular Fundraising Committee, suggested that the CFC look at a proposal that her committee had received in February but to which it had not responded because of a full slate of activities. That proposal was sent by Sharon McMillan, on behalf of her father Alvin French, who along with some of his buddies had been kicking around the idea of a golf tournament among African Canadians. Although not a JCA member at the time, Alvin thought that this organization would be the best vehicle through which to realize that dream.

On behalf of the CFC, Erma took the proposal to the JCA Board and, having secured its approval, ensured that Alvin and friends came to a general meeting to help sell the proposal. The membership gave its support. JCA was about to embark on a new venture.

Inaugural Tournament

Since the CFC had other events planned (a Merritone Benefit Dance in January 2000, a Boonoonoonos Celebrity Brunch in February), a small Golf Committee was formed to manage the inauguration of the tournament. The members were Alvin French, Chair; Erma Collins, Board Liaison; Winston Earle; Ivor Harriott; Jeff Patterson: and Alton Telfer. A consultant, Frank McGrath of Golf Tournaments Inc., was hired to guide the inexperienced committee. The first tournament was held at the Bolton Golf Club on August 26, 2000, under the patronage of the Hon. Lincoln Alexander and His Excellency Raymond Wolfe, High Commissioner for Jamaica.

Sponsors that year were Jamaica Tourist Board, Air Jamaica, TraceData Services Inc., Brantville Construction, Regal Constellation Hotel, Moda Luci, CBM Group Ltd., Clublink, Krazy Krust Patties, Club Epiphany, and Nettlewoods. Other donors were Golf Tournaments Inc., the *Jamaican Observer*, the Jamaican Consulate, Nicey's Food Market, Don's Meat, Scent and Sensibilities, Tax Right, Malvern Town Centre, Councillor Sherene Shaw, Mary Anne Chambers, Erma Collins, Fred Debidin, Winston Earle, Alfred Hewitt, and Neville Morrison.

Over 100 golfers participated, including a contingent from Hamilton and a foursome from the Toronto Police Services. Jaipaul Suknana, winner of the Men's Low Gross, won a trip to Jamaica, courtesy of Jamaica Tourist Board and Air Jamaica. Pamela Lecky, winner of the Women's Low Gross, won a beautiful gift basket, courtesy of Nettlewoods. Every golfer got a prize, and people went away with the widest of smiles and with the request that the JCA "do it again." The only dissatisfaction was with the golf club menu.

Financially, we broke even. The consultant's fee was $4,280.00. The committee regarded that fee as the price of learning how to run a tournament and vowed to do so without a consultant in the future. However, to compensate for not making money at the tournament, committee members promoted and executed a winter dance in January 2001, netting about $12,000, part of which provided seed money for the next tourney.

Celebrities Launch JCA Golf Tournament

(l-r) Michael Lindsay; Alton Telfer, Herman Stewart, Hon. Lincoln Alexander, Jeff Patterson, Hon. Portia Simpson Miller, His Excellency, Raymond Wolfe.

Year Two: 2001

The Golf Committee was expanded from six to ten, with the addition of some experienced golfers: Karl Killingbeck (to whom Alvin relinquished the chair), Earl Lalor, Keith Mills, and Neville Miles. Among the new sponsors that joined the inaugural ones were Flow 93.5, Southport Data Systems, Grace Kennedy Foods, Brookfield Properties Ltd., Keybase Financial Group, Carby Denture Clinic, and Optimum Advantage Financial Services. Patrons were Consul General to Toronto Stewart Stephenson; Senator Anne Cools; and Mr. Denham Jolly, President of Flow 93.5. The tournament was held at the Cardinal Golf Club. Along with family members, friends, and volunteers, the 144 golfers who took part enjoyed Jamaican cuisine at the JCA centre, after the game. The profit that year was $7,795.00.

Year Three: 2002

In 2002, there was a tremendous increase in sponsorship and donors, from 38 corporations and individuals the year before to 52. Among the new sponsors were Sandals, Western Union, Wyndham Rosehall Resort, Mirabel Travel, Alta Nissan, Guinness Extra Stout, and Kedar Hair Design. Patrons were Consul General to Toronto Vivia Betton; MPP Alvin Curling; and Toronto's Commissioner for Economic Development, Joe Halstead. Also, a second woman, Adoama Patterson, joined the committee. There were 140 golfers. We netted $16, 595.00.

Year Four: 2003

Prior to the August tournament in 2003, there was another development. For a week in March, the committee held its **first winter-get-away golf vacation** at Sandals Dunns River in Jamaica. Sandals Resorts, Mirabel Travel, and Air Jamaica collaborated in providing an affordable and memorable vacation for those golfers and their families who availed themselves of the opportunity. The tradition continued for a number of years.

The 2003 tournament was slated for August 16th. On August 14th, there was a power failure that affected 10 million people in Ontario and 45 million in eight U.S. states. On the morning of the 16th, the Cardinal Golf Club was still unreachable by telephone. Each committee member prayed that enough golfers would turn up and pay (many paid at the club on tournament day) to prevent us from losing our hefty down payment to the club. Thankfully, 111 golfers turned up. The profit that year was $12,265.00.

The patrons were Consul General to Toronto Vivia Betton; Commissioner Joe Halstead; and Toronto Argonauts Football Club Head Coach, Michael "Pinball" Clemons. New sponsors included Appleton Jamaica Rum, Edward Jones Financial, Manhattan Golf Club of Rochester, Molson Breweries, Remax, and Speed Freight.

Year Five: 2004

There were 150 golfers in 2004, the last year in which this writer was directly involved. A profit of $11, 873 was realized. New sponsors that year were Senvia; RBC Financial Group; Keith Lyons, Denturist; Laparkan Sea and Air Cargo; and Owen Chambers and Associates. The patrons were Consul General to Toronto Vivia Betton; York South Weston M.P. Alan Tonks; Ontario's Minister of Colleges, Training, and Universities, Mary Anne Chambers; and *Toronto Star* columnist Royston James.

2005 and Beyond

In 2005, Keith Mills succeeded the very able Karl Killingbeck as chair. Although there have been fluctuations in attendance and sponsorship, the JCA's 12th Annual Golf Classic was held on August 13, 2011 at the Maples of Ballantrae Golf Club. FLOW 93.5, Appleton Estate Jamaica Rum, Grace Kennedy, Cabinets and Granite Direct, Rap's Authentic Jamaican Dishes, and Jamaica National were major sponsors of the 2011 event.

Conclusions

Each year after the first, a post-tournament reception has been held at the JCA Centre, where some have comfortably lingered until past midnight. Authentic Jamaican food (mostly catered by Jean McIntosh over the years), a prize for every golfer, auctioning of Caribbean holidays: these have been integral parts of the proceedings. These aspects have made the JCA tournament unique and prized by participants.

Renting a golf course and carts is a very expensive undertaking. Without the sponsors and donors, who have provided cash and prizes, JCA would have made no money. Without an organizing committee, as well as dozens of JCA volunteers at the course and at the centre on tournament days, there would be no tournament. Without the confluence of people and ideas in 1999, JCA would not have added this service to its roster, thereby introducing a whole different set of Jamaican Canadians, other Caribbean people, and politicians to the organization. The journey continues.

The Jamaican Canadian Association Women's Committee

(Authored by Daphne Bailey, Eunice Graham and Pamela Powell)

The Women's Committee of the Jamaican Canadian Association (JCA) is a permanent and continuous entity that is woven into the fabric of the Association.

The Committee was initially established in 1975 as the Women's Auxiliary, in response to social change in the larger community as it related to women's issues. After operating successfully for three years the group became dormant.

In 1988 the group was re-established as the Women's Committee under the leadership of Eva Smith who was instrumental in reactivating the group so as to deal with the issues of particular concern to women.

On January 20, 1988, a core group of women met to discuss reorganizing the women's group. The outcome of the meeting was very positive, generating a great deal of interest, excitement and anticipation to regroup quickly. The officers were Eva Smith, Chairperson, Theo Brisco, Vice-Chair, Eunice Graham, Secretary and Lorna Muir, Treasurer.

Women's Committee Launch

On April 30, 1988, the group held a Wine and Cheese Reception to officially launch the JCA Women's Committee. Dr. Mavis Burke was invited as special guest. She was unable to attend but she sent a congratulatory letter in which she mentioned the "need to provide a resource to identify the problems being experienced by our women and to facilitate solutions to specific situations." She emphasized the fact that "many reports highlighted the stress of working conditions for women, the breakdown of the family, violence in the home and related problems." These are some of the issues to be addressed by the Women's Committee.

Three specific objectives were stated for the Women's Committee at its inauguration.

- To provide a forum to address women's issues and to be a support and resource group;
- To initiate special projects and to provide an avenue for networking with women of all ages;
- To assist in the fundraising efforts of the JCA.

In 1988 activities planned and executed by the Committee included:

- Trip to Shaw Festival (August 20)
- Seminar on Employment Equity (cancelled due to Hurricane Gilbert)
- Bazaar at 658 Vaughan Road
- Donation of educational toys to the Jamaican Consulate (December 9)
- Investigation into the declining number of Caribbean Domestic Contract Workers
- Assistance to three families with contribution of food and toys

In 1989 the Committee celebrated International Women's Day. The guest speaker was Judge Pamela Appelt, who spoke on the topic "Black Women in History."

The Committee held a Parenting Session with panelists Veronica Hislop, Zenova Brown, George Martin and Karl Oliver. The focus of their presentation was the comparison between parenting styles in the Caribbean and North America. A trip was planned to the Museum of African-American History in Detroit. There was also a Bazaar and Book Sale at the end of the year.

Over the ensuing years, the Women's Committee remained involved in planning and implementing a range of activities and events covering a variety of issues impacting women generally, and black women in particular. Some of these included housing, health care and violence against women.

Black Women's Health Fair

On November 20, 1993 the Committee held the First Black Women's Health Fair. The Health Fair was unique as this was the first of its kind in Canada by a black community organization. The theme of the fair was "Black Women Taking Care of Their Health". Funding for the project was accessed from the Ontario Women's Directorate, Anti-Racism Secretariat and the Women's Health Bureau of the Ministry of Health. The major aim of the Fair was to raise awareness of black women and their families about health issues and the impact of societal factors on their health. The Health Day featured a keynote speaker who spoke on black women's health, issues that impact our health, followed by a panel discussion with audience participation. Attendees were invited to visit information booths where resource people were available to give information on relevant health issues. A mobile health unit was provided where participants could have their blood sugar and blood pressure tested.

The Fair was extremely successful and very well received with an attendance of over 200. Special guests included representatives from the various ministries that funded the project, Ontario Human Rights Commission, Member of Provincial Parliament and the Consul General of Jamaica to Toronto.

The Black Women's Health Fair was the beginning of a long-term strategy by black women in the province to take charge of our health. It established fundamental rights of black women to control the process. This was a change from black women giving up their rights and always taking care of everyone else. We continued to fulfill our mandate by addressing women's issues in the form of seminars, workshops and fora, collaborating with other groups on relevant topics including, mental health, diabetes and hypertension. Over the years the Women's Committee has been evaluating its work; and in its endeavour to remain relevant and effective, the Committee has evolved its work to include a more global perspective of the plight of women and black women in particular. We are not disconnected from what is happening globally; the experiences we face here are connected to the experiences of women in other parts of the world. This has led the Committee to develop a 5-Year Action Plan in 1998.

Five-year Action Plan

The 5-Year Action Plan was framed in the context of the United Nations, "Platform for Action" (PFA) which was adopted at the Fourth World Conference for Women, held in Beijing, China in 1995. At this Conference, the PFA was adopted by the 189 member states of the United Nations, (including Canada). The actions to be taken by governments constituted 12 critical areas of concern affecting the equality rights of women and the girl child.

The objectives of the Plan were:

- Politicizing Committee members in terms of political education and development from a gender-based perspective;
- Education of the Membership and Board on gender equity issues;
- Critical analysis and assessment of women in the organization;
- Identify and implement strategies to promote women in power and decision-making;
- Introduce gender equality as part of JCA's policies.

The Committee achieved its objectives through seminars, fora, workshops, conferences, round table discussions, film presentations and discussion: Some of the topics covered were: Prostate cancer with urologist, Dr. Gervais Harry; Violence Against Women; Black Women and Men, Building a Community Based on Equity; Planning a Path for Women in the New Millennium; The Role of Women in the JCA and the Wider Community; Colorectal and Breast Cancer; Women and the Environment; Women and the Economy; Women and Poverty; Atrocities Against Women; Diary of a Mad Black Woman; Miss Amy and Miss May, Mary Secole—The Jamaican Nightingale, Water; Blood Sisters; Journey to Justice.

International Women's Day

Since March 5, 1998 the Committee has participated in the International Women's Day (IWD) celebrations sponsored by Women's Intercultural Network (WIN). Each year the organization presents two awards (IWD and Dr. Vara P. Singh). Joan Grant-Cummings, a Committee member, was the recipient of the International Women's Day Award in 1998. Sandra

Carnegie-Douglas, another Committee member, received the Vara P. Singh Award in 2000. Amy Nelson received the IWD Award in 2001 and in 2009 Pamela Powell received the Vara P. Singh Award.

In 1999 the Committee reviewed its Mission Statement, which reads: **"The Women's Committee of the JCA will work to advance women's full participation and equality in all aspects of the JCA and the wider community; including decision-making and leadership roles".** Its Goals and Objectives, Terms of Reference/Code of Ethics; Mechanisms for Supporting Women's Committee Chair on JCA's Board of Directors were also developed. These are reviewed on a regular basis. From 1988 the group operated as a non-standing Committee carrying out its mandate and it was not until 1999 that the Committee gained representation on the Board as a voting member.

Research Project

Between 1999 and 2004 the Committee participated in research projects as follows:

The Caribbean Women's Cancer Study sponsored by the Toronto Hospital Women's Health Program. The study investigated barriers to cancer screening among older women from the Caribbean living in Canada.

Women as Volunteers, The Unique Journey in Self-Empowerment and in Building Communities (Celebrating the Contributions of Women in the Community). The study was conducted by Dr. Inez Elliston. The JCA Women's Committee served as the Working Group in the development of the survey instrument and encouraged their members and other women volunteers in the Association to participate in the study.

Women Recognizing Women

On March 19, 2000, the Women's Committee held its first annual International Women's Day Celebration. Our guest speaker was Dr. Inez Elliston who told the distinguished gathering that "we need to publicize and promote our accomplishments more widely and put it into perspective for the main stream community to appreciate, respect and accept the good work you are doing". A segment of the program was dedicated to honouring past and present women volunteers of the JCA. They were awarded with the "Women Recognizing Women" certificate. This recognition has continued to be part of our annual IWD celebration.

Women's March in Ottawa

In 2000 the Committee participated in the World March of Women in Ottawa, Canada by spearheading the "Black Women's Coalition." A group of Black women's organizations formed a contingent and participated in this event to address violence against women and poverty. It was estimated that over 10,000 people attended the march. The purpose of the march was to draw attention to the inaction by governments regarding the actions agreed to at the Beijing Conference in 1995 to improve the conditions of women worldwide.

In 2001 to 2010 the Committee continued its mandate by addressing women's issues and providing educational sessions to the membership and community. These included a conference titled "Free Trade Areas of the Americas" (FTAA), in November, 2001. A panel consisting of William (Bill) Graham, Chairman of the Standing Committee on Foreign Affairs and International Trade, June Veecock, Trade Unionist and Director of Human Rights at the Ontario Federation of Labour, Sandra Carnegie-Douglas, Executive Co-ordinator of the National Action Committee on the Status of Women, and Ray South, Director of Southport Data System addressed the audience on the pros and cons of the proposed Free Trade Agreement.

"Women and the Environment" in June, 2009. The guest speaker was Dr. Ann Phillips. Her presentation focused on "mobilizing our community and healing ourselves". The presentation was followed by a panel discussion.

In 2010 another conference was held, titled "Women and the Economy". Four speakers dealt with Real Estate, Family Law, Life and Critical Care Insurance and Retirement Strategies.

The Committee was involved in other projects such as:

- Development of the video "Violent Night" which deals with the issue of domestic violence, particularly in the black and Caribbean community.

- Representation on the committee that produced the JCA 40th Anniversary video—"JCA, Its Founders, Its Legacy, 40 Years of Caring & Sharing."
- Alzheimer Society "Coffee Break" fundraising drive
- Beechcroft Women's Project in Jamaica

Current involvement includes:

- Contributes to the JCA newsletter, *InFocus* by publishing articles in the Women's Space section, highlighting women who have made significant contributions to the empowerment of women.
- Some members of the group adopted a child in Africa.
- Donations to the Stephen Lewis Foundation, specifically to the Grandmothers Project.
- Support to Eva's Place annually by donating toiletries, clothing and cosmetics.
- Donations to PACE Canada.
- Community Gifting annually of clothing and toiletries to Women's Shelters and to young mothers and babies.
- Support to the Jean Augustine Chair at York University through monetary donations.

The Committee is comprised of a very vibrant, committed and dedicated group led in the past by Chairpersons Eva Smith*, Pamela Powell, Camille Hannays-King and currently Charmaine Sewell, supported by the following past and present members: Marilyn Amiel*, Bernice Bailey, Daphne Bailey, Theo Briscoe*, Zenover Brown, Marjorie Cameron, Ruby Collymore, Enid Collins, Joan Grant-Cummings, Norma Clarke, Haslene Davis, Sandra Carnegie-Douglas, Eunice Graham, Ena Harrison, Amy Henry, Rosemarie Hylton, Esther Marks, Ismay Murray, Amy Nelson, Lorna Plummer, Sheila Raymond, Kristy Salmon, Juliette Saunders, Raphaelita Walker, Jameleia Williams. *deceased.

The Caribbean Canadian Seniors Group

Caribbean Seniors as they Sing

Roy Williams is quoted in *InFocus*, April 23, 1986 "One of the key objectives to be achieved this year is the formal organization of a black and Caribbean seniors' club. Last year we did a research study on the needs of this group and pledged then that we would try to organize the group and set things in motion to begin to deal with the plight and concerns of our senior citizens in their golden years. We are looking forward to having this matter well underway by the time of our Annual Seniors' Dinner the first week in September.[52]"

The Annual Seniors' Dinner was inaugurated by President Rupert James on Sunday, November 14th 1982 at the Grant AME Church. It was always well attended by seniors and we could notice the significant increase in numbers year after year. It was hugely apparent that this ethno-cultural seniors' group needed a place of their own where they could relax, reminisce, play games, exercise, sing, dance, do arts and crafts, become computer literate, play domino and do whatever else pleased them, in comfort.

Veteran JCA members Alex Russell and Amy Nelson took the bull by the horns and began to organize Seniors' Days on successive Tuesdays and Thursdays between the hours of 11:00 a.m. and 4:00 p.m. They would recruit black and Caribbean seniors, starting with those from their own churches, and then expand to other churches; and they invited them to come to the JCA on those days. As time passed the word spread far and wide and more and more seniors showed up at the JCA Centre at 1621 Dupont Street.

From the very start it was apparent that this was not a passive group. Their programming includes arts and crafts, a seniors' choral group, discussions, speakers from time to time on issues of importance to seniors, seminars, field trips, spring and autumn bus trips, boat cruises and regular trips to the casino in the summer and autumn seasons. This group is so spry and active they put the regular JCA group members to shame. They are always on the go. They go on extensive ocean cruises and by now some have already sailed the seven seas or are close to doing so.

After Alex Russell's death in November, 1999 leadership of the group fell squarely on the competent shoulders of Amy Nelson who is ably assisted by Eulalee Smith, Loy Manning, Ruth Morris and others. They managed to keep the group functioning without missing a single beat as the JCA moved from Dupont Street to a new location. During the interim the Seniors conducted their activities at the following locations: 1122 Finch Ave West, Grand Ravine Community Centre and at a Church Hall on Eddystone Drive in North York. The group is now comfortably ensconced in its new home at 995 Arrow Road and they keep the place humming with activity from 11:am-4:pm every Tuesday and Thursday. Miss Nelson indicates that the greatest benefit that the group receives is the social contact as they are able to interact with their own ethno-cultural peer group and can establish and maintain friendships.

The seniors have developed a very proficient Choral Group that gives three major performances each year—at the Seniors' Dinner, at the Year End Break-Up function at Christmas time, and at the Black History Month event. They also perform from time to time at senior citizens' residences. They have also performed at City Hall. Miss Nelson remarks that "the seniors love to sing."

The seniors finance their own activities as they make small weekly contributions to take care of the refreshments, supplies and incidentals. They are also very ably supported in the planning and conduct of their various activities by their facilitator, Ms Tricia Lamey. It is an inspiration to watch them in action every Tuesday and Thursday as they busy themselves with bingo, domino, various table games and activities. Their numbers continue to increase at a steady pace. This is a product of the Jamaican-Canadian Association which continues to play a supportive role by making the space and other resources available.

Participants at a JCA Event

The North York Seniors' Health Center Family Advisory Committee

The North York General Hospital Seniors' Health Centre is one of the leading geriatric facilities in Canada. The 164 bed facility was created in 1985 to provide geriatric health care for Seniors who require higher levels of nursing care. In 1990 it expanded, adding another 40 beds specifically designed to serve the multi-ethnic community who do not have a facility of their own. These 40 beds were reserved—10 beds each to the Armenian, Ismaili Muslim, black/Caribbean and the Latin American Communities.

A Family Advisory Committee was created that consists of family members of the residents, staff from the Health Centre, and representatives from each of the four targeted ethno-cultural communities. The Jamaican-Canadian Association has participated in this effort since 1990 as the organization that represents the Caribbean and black community. The members who have served on this advisory Committee almost continuously since that time are Daphne Bailey, Amy Nelson and Linda Gray. The committee meets on the fourth Monday every month to discuss issues concerning the four communities.

The committee is chaired by a member of one of the ethnic committee representatives and the chair rotates among the four communities with each serving a one-year term as chair. Both Miss Bailey and Miss Gray have served as chair of the committee. Overall the main purpose of the committee is to share experiences and customs and educate the committee members and staff on the cultural—ethnic needs of all the residents in the nursing home.

Every year in the month of November the Advisory Committee organizes an education night for the residents, staff and family members. These deal with relevant issues, (e.g. Alzheimer's, Heart Health, and Fire Safety) and are often dramatized by actors from the Jewish community and also the Ryerson Players. In December Charles Dickens' "A Christmas Carol" is usually presented with the assistance of readers from the Canadian Broadcasting Corporation (CBC). In April each year there is a "Meet and Greet the Family" event that provides the opportunity to interact with family members and to answer questions posed by family members or other visitors. From time to time, in the fall, the Committee hosts a cultural evening for the residents.

This is a very worthwhile service performed by these three JCA women on behalf of the entire Caribbean and black community for these many years. They ensure that this space that has been secured for our aged seniors is protected. They ensure that their culture is respected, and they ensure that quality care is provided in an amicable environment.

The occupancy of late has been Ismaili Muslim 16, Caribbean and black 15, Armenian 13, Spanish 1, and Chinese 9. There is an expectation that the respective ethno-cultural communities will support the aged residents with regular and frequent visits as well as volunteering from time to time at the facility. The other communities have met this expectation. The Caribbean and black community has not done as well. We do need to show our faces at these facilities to encourage and support the residents, as well as the caregivers. The residents would be really pleased and encouraged by regular visits as well as volunteers from the Caribbean and black community.

"JCA Stalwarts Having Fun"

The JCA Saturday Morning Tutorial And Heritage Program

(Partial excerpt from Article by Dr. Sylvanus Thompson)

The Jamaican-Canadian Association (JCA) is aware that education is a life-long journey of learning and hopes that the very best possible education will lead our children to a world of opportunity and a future filled with academic and professional success. The Association is therefore committed to delivering programs that promote and sustain the academic achievements of Caribbean and African children. The Saturday Morning Tutorial and Heritage program (SMTP) is one such program.

The SMTP was conceived in 1991 while Herman Stewart was chairperson of the Education Committee. He, Janet Neilson, Executive Director, and Billroy Powell, Program Coordinator, formed an ad hoc group to develop the tutorial program to offer "remedial classes that will assist students who are experiencing difficulties learning at school and in need of additional support"[53]. The goals of the program were:

- To prepare students to be more enthusiastic about education.
- To assist students to develop confidence so that they adopt a more positive approach to learning
- To provide an opportunity for more individualized learning, due to smaller student group learning.

"The program, which was developed for Black Youths aged 7-13 years old, started in January, 1992, and included remedial classes in English, Mathematics, Black History, Arts and Craft and Recreational activities."[54]

The SMTP currently falls under the jurisdiction of the JCA Education and Cultural Committee. It is a weekly program that runs from 10:00 a.m. to 1:00 p.m. on Saturdays during the school term for students from Grades 1-12, who are in need of additional support to meet their educational standards and goals. The program primarily focuses on English language and mathematics skills and homework assistance. This is supplemented by special workshops and educational field trips. The annual Career Counselling workshop, which is done in collaboration with INROADS, is open to students from the wider community, and is an example of such activities.

The students are also exposed to various cultural activities as a part of the cultural heritage component of the program. Parents and other interested persons are welcome to participate in the various cultural activities. Furthermore, in recognition of the important supportive roles of the parents, the program includes parent orientation sessions with specially invited guests covering a wide range of topics on the education system. Parents are also kept informed of the various activities.

"The JCA is proud of the fact that it has been able to create a supportive environment to facilitate youths in the community in meeting their educational goals. Its success is mainly due to a dedicated and committed group of volunteer tutors, comprised of current and retired teachers and other professionals of various disciplines, who run the program. In order to accommodate the growing demand for the program, additional volunteers are being sought. Volunteering is fun, personally rewarding and provides the opportunity to spend valuable time with young people who can appreciate and benefit from real world experience. Target groups include students seeking degrees in education, who can earn practicum experience, current and past educators; Grade 10-12 students can serve their 40 hours of community service mentoring younger students; and any other professionals or non-professionals who want to make a difference within the community.

The SMTP is a valuable community program that relies on many groups to be successful including; the students, tutors, the parents, and the JCA Board, staff and membership. We invite you to play a part in this initiative."[55]

JCA Saturday Morning Tutorial Students and Staff

Dr. Vincent Conville Teaches at the STMP

The Jamaican Canadian (Toronto) Credit Union Limited

The JCA established its own credit union in 1963 and it functioned successfully for 30 years until it reorganized in 1993 to form the Caribbean Canadian African (Ontario) Credit Union Ltd. During those 30 years it was the major financial institution owned and managed by members of the black community in Toronto and in Ontario.

The credit union is a co-operative financial institution owned by its members and it is managed by its members. It is capitalized by its members who save, both by acquiring and owning shares, as well as saving in the credit union. It then turns around and lends money, as needed, at nominal rates of interest to its members, based on the amount of their share holding and savings. Because of its low overhead, due to all the services being rendered by volunteer members, the spread between the interest charged to borrowers and the interest cost to the credit union enabled the credit union to turn a profit on the amount of money loaned during the year. At year end the Board of Directors is able to declare a dividend of a certain percentage to the shareholders, proportional to their shareholdings. Thus the money was saved, loaned, interest received and interest and dividends in turn paid back to the shareholders.

The credit union was a member of the Ontario Credit Union League which supervised and ensured the integrity of member credit unions and their operations. Members' deposits were insured with the League, and the League determined the percentage amounts of money to be held in reserve. It was in fact a properly regulated miniature banking system.

The Jamaican Canadian (Toronto) Credit Union Limited was managed by a Board of Directors consisting of a president, a vice president, a treasurer and two other members. Loans were processed by a Credit Committee consisting of three members whose job was to review each loan application and determine whether to approve or reject the application based on predetermined criteria and the credit worthiness of the applicant. Then there was the Supervisory Committee that pretty much functioned as the Internal Auditor that ensured that loan applications were in accordance with the by-laws and that the collection, deposit and disbursement of funds were likewise correct and in order. The credit union each year held an Annual General Meeting at which it reported to its members on the operation during the past year, presented plans for the coming year, and received the Supervisory Committee's reports. It also elected officers and committee members for the ensuing year.

Each year's activities was usually capped with a Gala Credit Union Dinner and Dance which in addition to the fun and frivolity often provided additional funds for the credit union's coffers.

During the years of the credit union's operations many persons developed skills in financial management and advising as they processed loans, encouraged savings and thrift, and counselled members on personal financial management. They facilitated the development of an economic vehicle that encouraged the circulation of money within the black community as well as capital accumulation therein. They could approach a loan applicant with special ethno-cultural sensitivity as the persons were sometimes known to them personally. Members felt more at ease approaching their own organization for loan than going to a bank or finance company which tended to be more impersonal and insensitive. In addition many new immigrants had little or no credit history and were more likely to be rejected or treated more harshly by traditional financial institutions in terms of harsher financial scrutiny, greater demands for collateral and co-signers, and finally higher interest rates. (Do not forget that race also may subtly enter the decision process.) Finally it was easier to approach and obtain a small loan from one's own organization than from the traditional institutions.

A 1992 Annual report of the credit union showed Cash Accounts totaling $107,329, Investments $2,911. Net Loans Receivable $188,681, Net Fixed Assets of $6,163, Other Assets $3,660 resulting in Total Assets of $308,744. Liabilities totalled $54,000, Share Deposits $231,188, Share Capital and Reserves $9,235 and Total Undivided Earnings $14,000. This shows a very healthy, strong financial condition. During the year they approved 30 of the 34 loan applications received totalling $85,650, with an average loan being around $2,855.

The above figures notwithstanding, the Board revealed that 1992 was not as good a year when compared to previous years due to the recession which had created severe hardships for some of their members. This resulted in job losses, layoffs, short work weeks and even bankruptcy for some members. Many members were unable to make their loan payments which resulted in the highest level of delinquency in many years. The

Credit Committee reported fewer loan applications compared to previous years. Despite all of the above, the Board still was able to declare a three per cent (3%) dividend on shares, based on a minimum quarterly balance.

Pressure to reorganize

In the early 1990's there was intense pressure coming from certain elements within the NDP Government at Queen's Park to eliminate small credit unions. This would be accomplished by mergers with larger credit unions or by expanding the bonds of association, thus expanding the potential membership base. Some government funding would be provided to facilitate the transition to the newly formed Caribbean African (Ontario) Credit Union Ltd. This transition for the new credit union required moving into a rented store front location, opening six days per week, at least 9:00 a.m. to 5:00 p.m., with salaried staff and a full time manager just like a regular bank. The volume of business just was not there to support that level of overhead expenses.

In addition the synergy was not there. Whereas the membership formerly was homogenous, the new heterogeneous membership had the potential for greater conflict and controversy. Some of the potential new members knew nothing about credit unions and their operation. Furthermore some of them thought that the government had given money to the credit union to distribute to the black community and they would show up demanding their share.

Expanded Membership Base

In 1992 the JCA credit union amended its Bonds of Association (Membership) from "Members of the Jamaican-Canadian Association Inc. within the Municipality of Metropolitan Toronto" to include "Persons from the Caribbean Community and persons of African ancestry (born in Canada or elsewhere) residing in the Province of Ontario." This greatly expanded the catchment area and the cultural communities from which new members could be drawn, but it also sowed the seeds of conflict.

The Jamaican Canadian (Toronto) Credit Union Limited was dissolved and the new Caribbean Canadian African (Ontario) Credit Union Ltd. was established on July 20, 1993. It was short lived. Within two years it was wound up by the Ontario Credit Union League. The League continued to collect the outstanding loans, paid off the liabilities, and distributed the remaining assets to its shareholders.

A Devastating Loss

It was a sad day for the Jamaican-Canadian Association who had birthed, then parented this credit union for 30 years. It was a sad day for the black community which had now lost the only black owned and black managed financial institution in Toronto and probably Ontario. It was a sad day for members and shareholders of the credit union which had served them so compassionately over the past 30 years. It was a sad day for the officers and directors who had now lost an institution which they had so lovingly and faithfully built over 30 years—Byron Carter, Alton Telfer, Neville Walters, Raphael Walters, Loy Manning, Eulalee Smith, Ismay Murray, Hermine Johnson, Barbara Schloss, Joyce Myers, Grace Williams and countless others who had served on the Board of Directors, the Credit Committee and the Supervisory Committee. It was a SAD, SAD DAY for all. Attempts to revive or start a new credit union have not been successful.

"Walkathon Participants at the Starting Gate"

JCA Domino Club

Wherever Jamaicans are gathered domino seems to be the table game of choice. Likewise at the Jamaican-Canadian Association domino is popular, both by the seniors and the juniors. It is most popular with the men but is also played by an increasing number of female afficionadas. It is a popular pastime after work hours and on weekends. As the male members of the Association ages, more of them retire and they now have more time for recreational activities. They needed to transform the sporadic pick-up games into a more formal format.

The late Josh Thompson and David Sinclair were avid domino players at the Excelsior Fraternal Society where there was an active domino club. However by 1985 the JCA had acquired its own building at 1621 Dupont Street and there was the space and available time slots for a variety of activities. It was not long thereafter that the formal JCA Domino club was launched with the late Josh Thompson as President and David Sinclair as Vice-President. Other individuals were selected as secretary and treasurer. Competitive teams were formed and Friday nights became the official JCA domino night.

In addition to the internal competitive teams there are excursions and tournaments from time to time. As early as 1985 there was an excursion to Montreal to engage in friendly competition with The Jamaican Canadian Association Domino Club of Montreal. These excursions entail spirited domino competition in the day followed by dinner and dance in the evening which capped off the friendly inter-organizational interaction. In course of time the visit was returned by the Montreal teams who were then hosted in like manner by the JCA Toronto Domino Club. In the early days this was an annual ritual.

Currently the JCA Domino Club meets regularly on Friday evenings in the Members' Lounge. They are a spirited group who seem to thrive on the competition and the camaraderie. They are ably organized and supported by Mrs. Josephine Spence, one of the officers of the club. They pay fees to support the club's operations and they purchase food and drinks provided. This is an active group that blends competition with partying as the DJ spins familiar tunes that encourages the non-players to display their creative talents on the dance floor. From time to time they make cash donations to the JCA, part in compensation for the use of the space and part as a contribution to the JCA's overhead expense.

Gifford Walker and JCA Domino Club players

The JCA Stalwarts

This book would not be complete if we did not devote a segment to the people of the JCA who make things happen. The JCA stalwarts. In the final analysis they are the principal reason the JCA has survived these 50 years. I think it was the Dofasco Steel Company in Hamilton, Ontario which had as its slogan "Our product is steel our strength is people." This slogan is never more apt than for the people at JCA. Indeed its strength is its people. We are talking about people whose lifelong commitment and devotion has been to the JCA. We are talking about people who gave literally thousands of volunteer hours to make sure the JCA challenges were met and to ensure the JCA survived.

It is impossible to list all of the stalwarts and we regret and apologize for those not mentioned and those who are mentioned are not mentioned in any priority order. They are simply people who come to mind. One of those is Sheila J. Simpson, C.A. the first chartered accountant from the black community who gave literally dozens of pro bono hours into the late nights at the JCA to set up our accounting so that the books could be properly audited and we could give credible financial reports to our funders and our members. She so very wanted our black community organization to be credible and to succeed. She didn't bill us because we could never pay her, and when she had to leave to go to the U.S. to join her husband she ensured she found and recommended a successor who would ensure that this black community organization would not fail or be tainted by financial malfeasance. Then there is Cyndi Anderson, the treasurer, who would be at the JCA offices way past midnight on so many occasions to ensure that the applications for funding or the reports to be submitted to the funders were correct and on time. In the dead of night and alone she would lock up and head for her house in Scarborough or Mississauga in time to get a few hours sleep before appearing wide eyed and fresh faced at her day job. Cyndi typifies so many others (women) who did the same thing, Hyacinth Wilson, Sheila Raymond, Barbara Thomas and others.

Who can forget Frank Wallace, a charter member of the JCA? He never owned a car. He lived way out in the suburbs accessed primarily by public transport. He assigned himself the role of care, keeper, and operator of the music, the equipment and the public address system at the JCA. He saw it as a personal responsibility to be there for every function. He felt that he was needed even if he had to run to catch the last bus that would take him home if he could not hitch a ride with someone who lived in that general neighborhood. He had a wife and two sons, one of whom had a disability. This he did after serving many years as the Association's Treasurer. He was a lifelong member of JCA until he died in 2009.

How about Gifford and Raphaelita Walker? They were early members of the Association and undertook to be the perennial Mr. and Mrs. Santa Claus for the Children's Christmas Party. In addition their Jamaica Government connection (Hon. Babsy Grange) has kept us in good stead with officialdom as Raphaelita has always maintained inside connections with the Consuls and Consuls General to Toronto. In addition they maintain high standing in the domino playing community.

Alton Telfer, ever present, ebullient, the greeter, the communicator, always undertaking challenging tasks—The Building Committee, the Trustee, Fundraising Committee, the Walkathon, the Golf Tournament. He is always there wanting to make a difference. He has donated trophies when and where he thought trophies were warranted. He has served also as President of the Credit Union, and on the Toronto Police Commission's Black Consultative Committee. Alton Telfer is always there. He takes the time from his business ventures, his political activities, other charitable commitments and busy travel schedule to be a true JCA Stalwart.

Eva Smith is legendary. She started the outreach to young people in the school system. She was on the ground and observed what was happening to them. She knew something had to be done and she did it. She also reached out to the women on the Domestic Workers Scheme and tried to bring succor to their situation. She was a mighty force within the JCA often challenging the JCA to be brave, bold and proactive. Eva has no equal when it comes to community outreach. She does not wait for the lame and wounded to find her. She goes and finds them. She has been permanently memorialized by the Annual Eva Smith Bursary.

Alex Russell—there from the beginning. A calm and quiet voice of reason and wisdom. He was no firebrand yet forceful and convincing. He worked hard to help the JCA acquire its buildings and was one of the architects for the now vibrant Senior Citizens group. A JCA stalwart to the day of his death. Russell was typical of other JCA men, the late Roy B.A. Stewart, and the late Josh Thompson. They too were solid, faithful, long-term supporters and upholders of the JCA banner.

Erma Collins an organization resource par excellance. From the 1960s almost continuously through to the 2000's she has served in about every office in the JCA except that of president. Vice-President, Executive Secretary, Education Chair and others. She is competent, precise and thorough. Any task she undertakes has been completed at a level above the ordinary. She is calm, rational and non-egoistic. She is seen as the voice of wisdom and is often called upon for other assignments utilizing her academic qualifications. She has served on task forces, constitution committees, employment interview panels, Golf Committee, Capital Fundraising Committee and as parliamentarian. She has served the JCA with distinction.

Bruce McDonald, Leon Sutherland, Doug Robertson and Owen Dunbar compared to those previously mentioned these men are relative newcomers, but you would never know it. They saw the JCA as their own, their home and set to work right away. Bruce championed the Fundraising Committee and the Walkathon with vigor while Leon has taken the Building as his portfolio and what would the Association do without Doug Robertson. He sees everything that needs to be fixed in order to keep the building functioning. He doesn't wait for permission to fix it. He just does it outside and inside. Owen has chaired the Building Committee, continues to serve on that committee and has special care for the bar and its operation. They maintain outside the building and decorate the building with Christmas lights. They also decorate inside for the various functions including the New Years' Eve party.

Byron and Vie Carter were JCA starters and served the Association well for many years. Vie was on the first Executive and later served on other committees. Byron served as Vice President and chair of other committees, primarily the Social Committee. Byron spent a lot of his time away from his personal construction contracting business in order to volunteer to help renovate the buildings acquired by JCA. They have been members for their entire lifetime since the formation of the Association. Byron has also served as president of the Credit Union.

Neville Walters, Raphael Walters—both brothers worked hard on various committees of the JCA. Neville served for a time as Vice President. They also were heavily involved with the Credit Union—Neville as President and Raphael on the Credit Committee. They remained stalwart JCA supporters while they were still able.

Carmen Jens—A more devoted JCA person than Carmen is really hard to find. She served as Executive Secretary and in many other positions especially in those lean years when the JCA had few facilities and nothing was computerized. Recording, reproducing and circulating information in those days was not an easy task.

Fay and Vincent Conville—having mentioned elsewhere the people who served as presidents I decided not to devote this section to presidents, but Fay and Vincent as a team has to be mentioned. They are stalwarts in the areas of walkathon, fundraising and education and scholarship efforts. They have championed in these areas over the years and Vincent and Fay have to be commended. Whereas many past presidents have walked away after they turned over the gavel Vincent has remained engaged. He has worked very hard on the Walkathon, the Education and Scholarship Committee and the Saturday Morning Tutorial Program.

A special trio of stalwarts is Bernice and Daphne Bailey and Pam Powell. These sturdy ladies have been there from the early years and they are still looking good and going strong. And have they served the JCA well? So many committees on which they served. Membership, Fundraising, Walkathon and others. In addition to internal JCA committees Daphne has served on the North York General Hospital Seniors Health Center Family Advisory Committee since its inception in 1990. She with Amy Nelson and Linda Gray are the black/Caribbean Community's voice at the facility. Pam Powell has served on the Board and on many committees and for many years had been a dynamic force as Chairperson of the JCA Women's Committee. She has given strong leadership as the group has become an influential and potent voice within the JCA. This trio has been valuable and productive.

Janet Neilson—she does not seek the limelight but she volunteers for the JCA. She served as Executive Director in the days when there was not the large salary attached to the position. She had the ability to do research, needs assessment, creative responses to request for proposals, timely reporting to funders and general understanding of the Social and Community issues. She still volunteers with the Walkathon team.

The women who worked in the kitchen when we used to do Caravan and when we did our own catering for functions held at the Centre (mostly at Dupont Street). They cooked, they cleaned, they washed dishes and did all the grunt work that needed to be done in order to make us look good out front. They are many, and many of their names I am not remembering but every one of them is a hero and they are all stalwarts. Some did not have time to go home and dress up to attend the functions. They stayed in the background, and even today there are those like Mr. Herbert Green who does his magic from the kitchen and is not often hailed for his performance in preparing delectable eats. And Ken Walters who gives up his Friday and Saturday nights to work the Coatroom—all alone sometimes. These are selfless volunteer hours which often times go unacclaimed. They too are stalwarts.

Of more recent vintage we note Dr. Sylvanus Thompson. Despite his enormous responsibilities elsewhere and his frequent travel commitments he still finds time to render yeoman service to and for the JCA. He is relied on for all major decisions to be made by the board. He is responsible for labour relations, the functioning of the various committees; he serves on the Management Committee. He continues to be heavily involved with the Education and Scholarship Committee which puts on one of the biggest shows each year and he is still connected with the Saturday Morning Tutorial Program. He definitely has presidential potential. He would be a shoo-in should he choose to become available.

Pam Reynolds—Another of recent vintage seems to be always at the JCA. Always promoting membership when functions are proceeding in the various halls. It is an enormous task to keep track of members, their current addresses and phone numbers and to communicate with them on personal as well as official matters. In recent years membership was merged with Social Committee, thus downloading more responsibilities and tasks to this area.

Amy Nelson the "Founder".—You thought I forgot her. Never. She has turned out to be the most durable and most energetic of the original members. She has been there from before Day I and she is still running in high gear. She has been instrumental in acquiring this building and has from time to time spent her own money to acquire equipment and utensils for the JCA. She is ever mindful of the state and condition of the building and works constantly to ensure that it is properly maintained. Without her watchful eye a number of things would have fallen through the cracks. She has been a long time chair of the Building Committee and currently she lovingly takes care of the JCA Seniors. She is a true stalwart, as is her compatriots Loy Manning, Ismay Murray and Eulalee Smith who loyally serve the seniors and previously the Credit Union. Amy reminds me that she is the only one of the official "Founders" who has been there for the entire 50 years without taking even a brief hiatus.

Sheila Raymond, I distinctly remember when she was membership chair, how she spent many a night and weekends attempting to computerize the JCA membership list. I had acquired the JCA's very first computer at an auction similar to the incident with the mimeograph machine back in the 1960's. None of our people at the time knew anything about computers. We decided the membership list was too unwieldy and it had to be computerized. We designed the first membership data base. We decided the number and sizes of the fields we would need for each record and in what priority and how the information could be manipulated to generate the desired outputs—mailing lists, membership renewals, number of years membership and so on. It was a gigantic task, especially for neophytes. Sheila labored at it putting in the data, night by night, name by name until we had the first JCA member database. Sheila has been steady at it for all those years chairing or being a member of various committees and task forces, the 40th Anniversary Organizing Committee and the JCA Women's Committee. Currently she is a key member of the very active Walkathon Organizing Committee. A true stalwart.

Barbara Thomas—Commitment, dedication, and hard work personified. She has served as a Vice-President of the JCA and Chair of

the Social and member of various other committees. During her tenure she was responsible for many of the JCA's major functions; she was the board member liaison with the Social Services sector and is currently still active with the Golf Committee and the Walkathon Committee. She is action oriented and ensures that what needs to be done gets done. Wherever and whenever there is a good deed to be done Barbara Thomas is there and she does not restrict her volunteering to the JCA Community. She is totally action oriented.

Joe Cross—Many may not remember Joe. He was so quiet and unassuming but a more dedicated and hard working JCA member you could not find. For many years Joe chaired the then Social Committee. It was active. It was vibrant. The JCA had many activities and its members had fun. Joe also served on other committees and was active until he migrated to the U.S.A. He still pays periodic visits to the JCA, of which he is still immensely proud.

Hyacinth Wilson and Francella Moore—both of these women served stints as chair of the Social Committee. Each in her own way moved the Association to new heights due to the attention they paid to details and the concern they had for the best interests of the members. They were active. The Association was active. Functions were well arranged. Attendance was high and people used to have fun. They were fun to be around. They each went way beyond the call of duty to ensure that the JCA succeeded. Hyacinth served a stint as Vice-President of the JCA and has served on the 40th Anniversary Organizing Committee and on many other committees. She is presently active on the Walkathon Organizing Committee. Francella, due to serious health issues is no longer active at the JCA but she gave it all she had when she was able.

There was a time when JCA participated in operating the bingo on Saturday nights to raise money at Finch Bingo Country on Finch Avenue West near to Weston Road. The bingo had to be manned/womanned by JCA members and volunteers. There was a team for each weekend in the month. That night was JCA's night and the team had to be there without fail. For as long as we had that Bingo not one team ever failed to fulfill its assignment. Talk about smoke-filled rooms. The bingo players smoked incessantly throughout the entire time. Your eyes burned from tobacco smoke. Your clothes smelled of smoke for an entire week. Through rain, sleet and snow the volunteers showed up. They each went way beyond the call of duty to ensure that the JCA succeeded. I do not remember all their names, but every one of them is a true stalwart.

There are countless other people who qualify as stalwarts but space does not permit a detailed listing. The above listed people are therefore a representative sample of hundreds of JCA stalwarts. Many arc listed in the appendix. The JCA could not have survived without them.

JCA Stalwarts

JCA Stalwarts at Caravan

Benefactors

The English poet John Milton
wrote in the last line of his sonnet "On His Blindness"
"They also serve who only stand and wait."

Denham Jolly

There are others in this community who serve in many other ways. The benefactors—they are hard-working entrepreneurs who have a business or businesses to operate. They cannot attend meetings, chair or serve on committees but they have the best interest of the JCA at heart and are committed to ensure that the JCA succeed. What can they do? They can place an advertisement in one or other of the JCA's programs or publications from time to time or on a continuing basis, and they do. They can donate cash from the profits that their businesses generate, and they do. The JCA has benefitted from the kind generosity of many benefactors—foremost among whom are Denham Jolly of Milestone Radio Inc., and Tyndall Nursing Homes Limited; Delores Lawrence of NHI (Nursing and Homemakers Inc.); Leila McKenzie of Park-Med Laboratories and Leisure World Nursing Homes Ltd. The Jamaica National Building Society, The Victoria Mutual Building Society and Western Union. These benefactors have served magnificently in the ways they best can. The JCA is eternally grateful.

Delores A. Lawrence

Reflections and Projections

Looking back on the first 50 years there is no doubt that the Jamaican-Canadian Association (JCA) has been both successful and effective. To have survived for 50 years is a monumental achievement. Organizations with a predominantly black membership base tend to rise, flourish for a few years and then vanish. The JCA started from nothing, with nothing, and methodically evolved to become the foremost organization in the black and Caribbean community in Toronto and Ontario.

To explain this longevity and survival one needs to look no further than the Association's original constitution and its nine stated objectives. Prominent among these objectives are:

- To better acquaint Canadians with Jamaicans' opinions on various matters.
- To mold the group into an effective and influential voice in community affairs.
- To co-operate with other groups in pursuing community aims and objectives.
- To establish a scholarship fund to assist Jamaican students in Canada.
- To give assistance to newcomers wherever possible.
- To establish a Centre for Social and Cultural Activities.
- To establish official contact with the Jamaican High Commissioner in Ottawa.

A performance evaluation based on the above objectives results in better than a passing grade—an A- to A+ range. That is very good to excellent; all of the above objectives have been achieved. Has it been an easy road? Information provided in the previous pages indicates that it has not been, but dogged perseverance and stick-to-itiveness has enabled these accomplishments.

Prominent also as an influencing element in the Association's survival is Nationalism and Patriotism. Jamaicans are proud of their country and their heritage. The JCA is an organization that supports, maintains and upholds the Jamaican traditions and national symbols with appropriate ceremony. Patriotic Jamaicans see the JCA as their anchor and they rally around events that elicit their patriotic fervour.

A further contributing factor to its survival was the newcomers need for affiliation and association with similar others, both to satisfy the human need for social relations and for facilitating the adjustment and adaptation process.

The JCA Success Formula

The longevity and survival formula of the Jamaican-Canadian Association is contained in the following:

(1) The vision of the "founders" that captured in the Constitution of the Association Overarching Values and objectives that remained valid for five decades.
(2) The character of its members (predominantly female) who remained constant and committed through periods of adversity as well as prosperity.
(3) The unparalleled Patriotism, Nationalism and Pride in being Jamaican.
(4) The High quality, selfless leaders and other volunteers who performed valiantly without expectation of tangible rewards.
(5) The fundamental commitment to democracy and respect for each individual.

The JCA as Successful Change Agent

Toronto, Ontario and Canada is a vastly different place than it was 50 years ago. The Jamaican-Canadian Association has played a vital role in its progression to be currently ranked by the United Nations as one of the best countries on earth to live. As the only black/Caribbean organization to have survived these 50 years it has, from the very beginning, raised its voice, petitioned, submitted briefs, demonstrated and spoke to all of the issues that affect the quality of life of the individual, especially that of the disadvantaged and voiceless.

There is a veritable shopping list of issues:

- **Non-racial Immigration Advocate.** Starting in 1963, with its first brief to the Minister of Immigration, Guy Favreau, and continuing in successive years the JCA relentlessly advocated for changes in Canada's Immigration Act, Regulations and Policies to make it non-racist, more humane and more accessible to all peoples, especially those of colour who were previously excluded.
- **Equal Employment Advocate.** The JCA was a continuing advocate and intervenor with the Ontario Human Rights Commission on behalf of hundreds of job applicants or employees who were denied employment, promotion or otherwise unfairly treated due to their color or race.
- **Equal Housing Advocate.** Vociferously advocated and intervened at the Ontario Human Rights Commission on behalf of housing applicants who were denied accommodation due to their race or colour. Conducted tests alternating with white and black applicants to establish the facts of racial or color discrimination.
- **Equal Access Advocate.** Strongly supported the right to access to public facilities without discrimination due to race or colour.
- **Fair Policing Advocate.** Frequent advocate before the Police Services Board for fair and equal policing. Represented many persons who were unfairly treated by police due to race or colour.
- **Community Policing Advocate.** Strongly advocated for a different brand of policing where police officers could be drawn from, and/or live in the neighbourhoods they policed. An alternative is a neighbourhood policing practice where police officers get to really know their neighbourhoods, and have frequent positive interactions with its residents. Thus resulting in improved Police Community Relations.
- **Anti Racial Profiling Advocate.** The JCA has always marvelled at the frequency with which black drivers have been stopped by police and postulated that racial profiling was being practiced. The JCA strongly advocates the discontinuance of racial profiling by the police.
- **Multi-Ethnic, Multi-Racial Policing Advocate.** The JCA has been a strong advocate for the recruitment of so called "visible minority" police officers to make the service more representative of the communities it serves, to better serve the respective

neighbourhoods and ultimately to dissolve negative ethnic and racial attitudes within the police service.

- **Equal Opportunity Promotion Advocate.** The JCA has always advocated that promotion be based on performance and ability rather than non job-related factors such as race or colour. As such so called "visible minority" and female officers would be found in all ranks throughout the police service. This has begun to bear fruit.
- **Civillian Oversight Advocate.** The JCA has been a long-time advocate that police cannot be their own investigator, jury and judge when dealing with police misbehaviour. They cannot be allowed to investigate themselves. The JCA has submitted briefs and made representations supporting Civillian Oversight Boards and the Special Investigations Unit (S.I.U.).
- **Child Education Advocate.** The JCA advocated and intervened with the North York, The East York and the Toronto Boards of Education in the education of Jamaican, West Indian and other immigrant children who were not in sync with the education system and its teachers. They innovated the Caribbean Outreach Booster Program, the Learning Enrichment Academic Program (LEAP) and the Saturday Morning Program to enable a proper fit between the children and the education systems.
- **Jamaican Teacher Accreditation Advocate.** Advocated for the acceptance of the Credentials of Jamaican trained and certified teachers in the Ontario education system.
- **Race Relations Policy and Training Advocate.** Advocated and served on various Race Relations Committees to assist officials and employees of various boards and institutions to eliminate racial attitudes and discriminatory behaviours from their establishments.
- **Employment Equity Advocate.** Strongly advocated for the Employment Equity Legislation that mandated that the population within organizations be reflective of their communities and the population in general at all organizational levels. That they not only employ but promote employees from the "designated groups."
- **Anti-Apartheid Advocate.** Advocated against the racist South African Government and recommended that the Canadian Government boycott and apply sanctions against that government.
- **Stigmatized Communities Advocate.** Advocated for Preventative and Support Programs to distressed and troubled communities

such as Jane-Finch and the inauguration of the Caribbean Outreach Project in the 1970's and 80s.
- **Multiservice Social Service Advocate.** Advocated for the establishment of the multiservice social agency (Caribbean Youth and Family Services) CYFS which has served thousands of distressed clients over the years.
- **Individual and Civil Rights Advocate.** Advocated for and represented hundreds of individuals in various situations when their civil rights or individual freedoms were violated.
- **Maintained Contact with the Jamaican Government** through the High Commissioner in Ottawa and the Consulate General in Toronto.
- **Toronto Consular office advocate**—Advocated vociferously with the Jamaican Government for the establishment of a Consulate in Toronto.
- Initiated and continued to celebrate annual Jamaican Independence and the Anniversary of the formation of the Jamaican-Canadian Association with the following events.
    - Flag Raising Ceremony
    - Church Service of Thanksgiving
    - Gala Independence Dinner and Dance
- Acquired three different buildings in sequence over the period.
- Been Disaster Relief Headquarters over the years for Hurricanes and Floods in Jamaica and earthquake in Haiti.

Challenges

Has the Association been perfect? No. Could the Association have been more successful? Probably. But the Association has done the best it could with the resources available to it; both in human and financial terms.

Human Resource Challenges

Until recently the JCA's management and activities were entirely staffed by volunteers. It is not always easy to get volunteers. Volunteers come with different levels of talent and abilities and different levels of commitment. Some volunteers' abilities are not, or cannot be properly matched to the tasks to be performed. Sometimes the talent is there but the commitment is missing. Sometimes it is the other way around the commitment is there but the talent is missing. Sometimes volunteers do not want to put in the time to become indoctrinated and to learn from the bottom up. Sometimes those who have learned from the bottom up are not willing to assume the responsibilities of leadership in the top positions. Sometimes volunteers want to go in only at the top position without taking the time to learn the inner workings of the position.

Formal training for any position or office does not exist. On-the-job learning, or learning by observation are the only learning methods currently available. The learning curve for anyone in an entirely new position is six to 12 months. The term of office for the position is usually two years. By the time the person is effective in the position his/her term of office is coming to an end. Should the person choose not to stay for a second term that knowledge and that learning walks out the door and the entire process has to be repeated with the new person if he or she comes in at the top of the ladder rather than promoted from within. One has to commit to at least 4 years (two terms) to really have an impact in the position to which one has been elected.

With no effective succession planning in place, with only on-the-job learning in place, and with the short term of office there is bound to be a reduced level of effectiveness for the entire organization. In addition, if there is an absence of stated policies, practices and standard operating procedures in place each new occupant of a position starts from scratch. He/she may spend time and energy attempting to reinvent a wheel which was previously invented or engaging in activities which had previously proved unsuccessful. This affects both efficiency and effectiveness.

The new century and new decade has so far marked the start of a new trend—the accession to high office within the JCA of persons with relatively short membership tenure. Prior to this all previous presidents had either been founding members or had been members of the JCA for many years. They had served on one or more of the Standing Committees and had assimilated the culture, traditions and values of the JCA. Post 2000 some presidents and other Board members had only recently joined the JCA. They did not really understand the JCA. They did not undergo an orientation and some had not previously served on any of the committees before being directly elevated to the board. They did not truly internalize JCA culture and traditions. Some barely completed their term in office and then they disappeared. Others did not last as long. There is much merit in requiring a specified number of years membership and service on one or other of the standing committees before assuming the highest offices in the Association. There is much evidence that without this some do not perform well and do not last long.

New people, new vision and new ideas are essential to the survival of any organization but these have to come from people who make a long-term commitment to the organization.

Forward to the Next 50

Going forward to the next 50 years, Human Resource Recruiting, Training, Development and Succession Planning for each position in the Association will constitute a major challenge. This is a challenge that must be addressed at an early stage as it may prove to be the Achilles heel that will inhibit the future growth or even survival of the Association. The Association has been fortunate so far. There is no guarantee that that luck will continue indefinitely.

Re-Inventing the JCA

Re-inventing the JCA is another critical matter. Some issues that come to the fore are as follows: The generation that created and sustained the JCA will come to the end of its lifetime within the next 10-15 years; the average age of the current membership is plus 55; the children of JCA members typically do not join the JCA; second and third generation Jamaicans do not share the same patriotic and national attitudes as their forebears; the annual inflow of Jamaican immigrants has decreased and is continuing to decrease; the major advocacy issues that the JCA has championed in the 1960's through to the 1980's have substantially receded; the settlement and adaptation services that the JCA once provided are now available through multiple sources; the social contact and meeting place facilities now exist in abundance and closer to their places of residence. There is no programming currently in place that encourages use of the premises by younger people. All of the above point to a reduced need for the JCA as it currently exists and the great need for a redesign to accommodate the new realities of a vastly changed environment, different demographics and the needs and desires of a different client base. There is a reason why some church and school buildings are empty.

Re-Imaging the JCA

Along with the Re-Inventing addressed above is the need to clarify the JCA image. Is it a socio-cultural, ethno-cultural organization, or is it a social service delivery organization, or is it both? Can it be both with optimum effectiveness to each? Can it be both fish and fowl at the same time? I contend that it cannot be. As of now the Social Service Delivery aspect has plateaued and has been so for some time. Little or no leadership has been shown there. There has been no innovation. There has been no growth. It is sometimes in trouble with its funders. It will continue to be so until it is severed from the JCA, and given its own wings so it can fly. It needs to have its own competent Board of Directors who knows some things about Social Services and Social Service Delivery. It needs a Board that can set policy, give directions and interact effectively with the Social Services Sector. The JCA also needs to go its own way and not be subject to the dictates of the funders for the Social Service Delivery Programs. Government funding is unreliable. Governments change, policies change and priorities change. There were painful examples of this in the 1990's when the Bob Rae NDP Government was defeated and Mike Harris' Conservative Government came to power (the Credit Union was lost, the Ebony Co-operative Housing was lost). The JCA should not allow itself to be solely dependent on government funding. Failing this the JCA will eventually lose its independence. This matter has been known for some time but it has been deliberately shelved by successive administrations, each of which was not willing to bite the bullet.

Building Membership

Building volume and quality membership is a natural outcome following the Re-inventing and the Re-Imaging referred to above. The JCA membership should be much larger than it currently is. In the Greater Toronto Area resides the largest Jamaican population and descendants of Jamaicans in Canada. "In 2001, 71% of all people in Canada who reported they had Jamaican ethnic origins lived in Toronto. In that year there were just over 150,000 people with Jamaican roots residing in Toronto where they made up 3% of the total metropolitan population[56]." By 2011 this population would be near or upwards of 200,000. The JCA membership should aim for at least 10 percent of that number. That would make for a healthy, wealthy and powerful association. It is achievable. It takes vision and leadership. It is a different demographic and must focus on youth and young people.

Building A Stable Financial Base

Critical to the JCA's survival into and through its next 50 years is its ability to do proper financial planning and budgeting. It is impossible to satisfy its vision and to accomplish its objective without the necessary funds to do so. Strategic Planning absent strategic Fundraising is a non-starter. There is a building to be maintained, improved or expanded. There will be (or should be) new programs and projects to be initiated. There are employees to be paid and increased emoluments and benefits to be dispensed. So far much of the above has been haphazard and project based resulting in suboptimal outcomes.

Organizations that survive do develop 5-year plans with a vision, objectives, time tables, performance measures, and associated human resource and financial budgets.

The JCA cannot continue to be so wholly dependent on government funding. Government funding should be reserved for the Social Service Delivery Sector and should go there when it has been severed. The JCA is no longer a toddler. It is a grown up organization and must learn to play in the grown up leagues. Its survival will depend on its ability to develop stable sources of long run funding. There are foundations, other funding sources and a large community base that have yet to be explored. Take a look at the Jewish community. Maybe it is time to take a leaf out of their book.

If the JCA is willing to seriously address the issues outlined above, it has the potential to move forward to the next 50 years that could possibly surpass the first 50.

Future JCA leaders

Notes

1. Moore, Donald, *Don Moore, An Autobiography* (Williams-Walker Publishers, Inc) Toronto, 1985, pg.144
2. Walker, James S.St.G. *The West Indians In Canada,* (Canadian Historical Association, Ottawa, 1984) pg.10
3. Ibid. pg. 9
4. Ibid. pg. 9
5. Armstrong, Bromley, L. *Memoirs of Bromley L. Armstrong,* (Vitabu Publications, 2000) p. 157.
6. Ibid. pg. 161
7. Ibid. pg. 162
8. General Purposes Committee Report, Sept. 1963
9. Walker, James S. St. G. *The West Indians in Canada,* pg. 9
10. Ibid. pg. 9
11. Armstrong, Bromley, L. *Memoirs of Bromley L. Armstrong,* (Vitabu Publications, 2000) pg. 161
12. JCA Monthly Reporter, August 1973
13. JCA Monthly Reporter, September, 1973
14. Manning, Williams, *My Name is Eva,* (Natural Heritage/Natural History, Inc.) Toronto, 1995, pg. 42.
15. JCA Treasurer's Report, 1977
16. Manning, Williams, *My Name is Eva,* (Natural Heritage/Natural History, Inc.) Toronto, 1995, pg. 22.
17. Ibid. pg. 23
18. JCA President's Report, 1980.
19. JCA Annual Report 1975, pg. 8
20. JCA Treasurer's Report 1980-1981-1982
21. Walker, James W. St. G.—*The West Indian in Canada* pg. 12
22. Armstrong, Bromley, L. Memoirs of Bromley L. Armstrong, (Vitabu Publications, 2000)
23. Moore, Donald, *Don Moore, A. Autobiography* (Williams-Walker-Wallace, etc.)
24. Hill, Donna, *A Black Man's Toronto,* 1944-1980, (Multicultural History Society Toronto, 1981)
25. JCA Balance Sheet December 31, 1983
26. JCA InFocus, May 1988

27. JCA Annual Report—1988
28. JCA Annual Report 1995-1996 pg. 1
29. JCA Annual Report 1995-1996 pg. 5
30. JCA Quarterly Report, March 10, 1996 pg. 5
31. JCA Annual Report 1995-1996 pg. 2
32. JCA Annual Report 2000-2001 pg. 3
33. JCA 37th Anniversary Program, 1999
34. JCA Annual Report 2000-2001, pg.2
35. JCA Annual Report 2001-2002 pg. 2
36. JCA Annual Report—2001-2002 pg. 4
37. JCA Annual Report—2001-2002 pg. 6
38. JCA InFocus, June 2004
39. JCA Quarterly Meeting, Nov. 3-, 2-3, Presidents Report, pg. 9
40. JCA Quarterly Meeting, Nov. 30, 2003, Presidents Report, pg. 10
41. JCA Annual Report, 2004-2005 pg. 3
42. JCA Annual Report, 2005-2006 pg. 5
43. JCA Annual Report, 1991
44. JCA Annual Report, 2000-2001, pg. 4,5
45. JCA Constitution, Sec. 41-4.6
46. JCA Annual Report, 1981, pg. 2
47. JCA Annual Report, 2001, pg. 3
48. JCA Annual Report, 2008-2009, pg. 13
49. In Focus, Winter 2011 pg. 4
50. (www.statcon.gc.ca/pup/89-621-x/89 The Jamaican Community in Canada)
51. JCA Treasurer's Report, 1981, 1982
52. JCA Annual Report, 1975
53. In Focus April 23, 1986
54. JCA Annual Report, 1991
55. JCA 46th Annual Independence Program, August 2008
56. (www.statcom.gc.ca/pup/89-621-x/89 The Jamaican Community in Canada)

Appendix 1

Table 1

Year	Number
1956	1245
1957	1414
1958	1360
1959	1369
1960	1340
1961	1307
1962	1659
1963	2443
1964	2281
1965	3215
1966	4133
1967	8582
1968	7755
1969	13315
1970	12660
1971	11017
1972	8353
1973	19563
1974	23885
1975	17973
1976	14842
TOTAL	159711

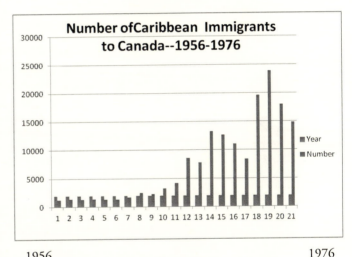

Chart 1

Statistics Canada, Table 075-008-Historical statistics, by Country of Last Permanent Residence, CANSIM (database)

Appendix 2

TABLE 2
JAMAICAN IMMIGRATION TO CANADA BY PROVINCE OF INTENDED DESTINATION AND BY SEX—1973-1996

Year	Total	Ontario	Quebec	Other	Total	Male	Female
1973	9363	8210	710	443	9363	4082	5283
1974	11286	9992	790	504	11286	4947	6339
1975	8211	7187	520	504	8211	4030	4181
1976	7282	6082	584	616	7282	3630	3652
1977	6291	5257	464	570	6291	3091	3200
1978	3858	3153	307	398	3858	1798	2060
1979	3213	2656	276	281	3213	1496	1717
1980	3181	2594	216	371	3181	1460	1701
1981	2553	2082	173	298	2553	1144	1409
1982	2593	2046	230	317	2593	1244	1349
1983	2423	1761	218	444	2423	1022	1401
1984	2479	1980	226	273	2479	987	1492
1985	2922	2465	202	255	2922	1185	1737
1986	4952	3937	409	606	4952	1742	2910
1987	5422	4744	461	217	5422	2277	3145
1988	3923	3400	304	219	3923	1809	2114
1989	3896	3376	289	231	3896	1910	1986
1990	4887	4294	316	277	4887	2354	2533
1991	4997	4489	200	308	4997	2324	2673
1992	5921	5415	188	318	5921	2640	3281
1993	5990	5425	246	319	5990	2736	3254
1994	3882	3490	127	265	3882	1808	2074
1995	3599	3284	112	203	3599	1664	1935
1996	3275	2981	113	181	3275	1522	1753
TOTAL	116399	100300	7681	8418	116399	52902	63179
PERCENT		86.20%	6.60%	7.20%	PERCENT	46%	54%

http://epe.lac-bac.gc.ca/100/202/301/Immigration Statistics-ef/index.html
http:/cic.gc.ca/English/resources/statistics/facts 2009/index.asp

Appendix 3

DRAFT OF NEW CONSTITUTION TO BE PRESENTED FOR APPROVAL TO MEMBERS OF THE JAMAICAN CANADIAN ASSOCIATION AT THEIR FIRST GENERAL MEETING – SEPTEMBER 23, 1962, AT THE Y.M.C.A., COLLEGE STREET, TORONTO.

PREAMBLE OF THE CONSTITUTION OF THE JAMAICAN CANADIAN ASSOCIATION.

We, Jamaicans living in Canada desiring :

1. To develop and maintain closer relations between Canadians and Jamaicans;
2. To better acquaint Canadians with Jamaican opinions (social, immigration, political, economical, racial, etc.);
3. To establish closer relations with Jamaicans living in Canada and to mold this group into an effective and influential voice in community affairs;
4. To co-operate with West Indians and other national or territorial groups, in pursuing common aims and objectives;
5. To provide a forum for noteworthy Jamaican speakers in Canada;
6. To establish official contact with the Jamaican High Commissioner in Ottawa;
7. To establish and maintain a scholarship fund to assist Jamaican students in Canada;
8. To give assistance to newcomers wherever possible.
9. To establish a Centre for social and cultural activities.

Do hereby adopt the following constitution.

ARTICLE I : NAME.

This organization shall be known as :

JAMAICAN CANADIAN ASSOCIATION.

Appendix 4

MINUTES OF THE FIRST EXECUTIVE MEETING OF THE
JAMAICAN-CANADIAN ASSOCIATION AT THE Y.M.C.A.,
COLLEGE STREET – SEPTEMBER 23, 1962.

Subsequent to the First General Meeting of the Jamaican-Canadian Association, the Constitution Committee met for the purpose of election of officers to the Executive.

The following are the officers :

- Mr. R. G. Williams — President.
- Mr. Bromley Armstrong — Vice-President.
- Mr. George King — Executive Secretary.
- Mr. Ira Dundas — Treasurer.
- Miss Mavis Magnus — Recording Corresponding Secretary.
- Mr. J. B. Campbell
- Mr. Owen Tennyson.
- Miss Phyllis White.
- Mrs. V. Carter.
- Mr. E. S. Ricketts.

Further appointments were :

- Mr. Bromley Armstrong — Chairman, General Purposes Committee.
- Mr. J. B. Campbell — Chairman, Education and Scholarship Committee.
- Mr. Owen Tennyson — Chairman, Publicity and Social Committee.

Appendix 5

Jamaican-Canadian Association Founding Members as of June, 1963

001–Adams, Fitzroy
002–Adams, Ms. Stella
003–Adolphus, Ms. B.
004–Anderson, Mr. R.C.
005–Anderson, Mr/Mrs. T.
006–Armstrong, Mr/Mrs. B. L.
007–Beckford, Ms Gloria
008–Best, Alfred
009–Black, B. & Mrs. C. T.
010–Black, Mrs. Lenna
011–Blake, Ms Olga
012–Bowers, Fred
013–Bennett, Ms Newton
014–Bailey, Mr./Mrs. C.
015–Bailey, Ms Bernice
016–Barker, George
017–Barrant, M. G.
018–Bailey, I. M.
019–Bailey, Ms Dorothy
020–Belnavis, L. S.
021–Brissett, V. E.
022–Brown, Mr. & Mrs.
023–Brown, Ms Gladys
024–Brown, Ms Avis
025–Brown, Ms C. M.
026–Brown, Mervin
027–Brooks, W.O.
028–Bryan, Evan S.
029–Butler, Ms Linda
030–Burt, Ms Inez
031–Bailey, Ms Joyce
032–Bradley, Ms B.
033–Bradley, ms Lois
034–Bradley, Mrs. Marion
035–Brammer, Ms Gloria
036–Braithwaite, A.
037–Bridge, Ms Y. A.
038–Callender, Mr. /Mrs. Victor
039–Campbell, Mr./Mrs. J. B.
040–Campbell, Ken
041–Campbell, Ms I. E.
042–Carter, Mr/Mrs. Byron
043–Carter, Ms Sylvia
044–Craig, H. A.
045–Cooper, Alex
046–Charles, Ms E.
047–Creed, R. S.
048–Clunes, Ms Thelma
049–Clarke, Ms Norma
050–Carey, Ms A.
051–Chambers, Ms P. E.
052–Chambers, Mrs. A.
053–Chambers, Ms. N. M.
054–Clayton, Ms M. R.
055–DaCosta, Frank
056–D'Aguilar, Donald
057–Dalrymple, Ms Laurna
058–Daley, Hugh
059–Davis, Ms Dorothy
060–DeSantos, Justin
061–Delfosse, Ms Arlene
062–Dixon, Mrs. Enid
063–Donaldson, Ms Cynthia
064–Douglas, Ms Adlyn
065–Douglas, Mr/Mrs. Lionel
066–Dundas, Mr./Mrs. I. W.
067–Dunn, Ms Cynthia
068–Dyke, Ms Carmen
069–Eubanks, Mr./Mrs. D. E.
070–Evans, Ms Marguerite
071–Ferguson, Ms C. B.
072–Fletcher, Neville
073–Fisher, Byron
074–Forbes, Ms N.
075–Frankson, Basil K.
076–Foster, Dr Dwight L.
077–Forrester, Claude
078–Galt, Ms Jean
079–Gardener, Ms Muriel A.
080–Garfield, Sylvan M.
081–Gatchair, Ms Marlene
082–Gayle, Ms Barbara
083–Grant, Mrs. Celeste E.
084–Goldberg, George S.
085–Grasser, William
086–Grant, Ms merle E.
087–Green, Clinton
088–Green, Edwin
089–George, Mrs. M.
090–Gray, Hector A.
091–Golding, Keith J. C.
092–Grizzle, Stanley G.
093–Hall, Ms Elsie
094–Harriott, Herman
095–Hutchinson, Ms Viola B.
096–Hurst, Howard
097–Hemming, Ms Evelyn
098–Howard, Ms Beryl
099–Henry, C. Donovan
100–Hill, Dr. Daniel G.
101–Heron, Louis O.
102–Heron, Roy
103–Hessell, Ms Pat
104–Hylton, Mr./Mrs. Gladstone
105–Henry, Ms Minette
106–Hastings, Athol
107–Ingram, Albert G.
108–Jackson, ms hyacinth
109–Jacobs, Dr. Allan A.
110–James, Ms Celia Ethnee
111–Johnson, Neville
112–Johnson, James
113–Johnson, Ms Lucille
114–Johnson, Ms Merlene A.
115–Jordan, Ms Marie
116–Keith, Ms Marjorie N.
117–Khan, Ms Lisa C.
118–Kirlew, John
119–King, Mrs. Agatha
120–King, Mr./Mrs. George

Jamaican-Canadian Association Founding Members as of June, 1963

121–King, Donald C.
122–Louithard, Joseph A.
123–Legge, B. J., QC
124–Leslie, Guy T.
125–Lewis, Ms C.
126–Lindo, Ms Daphne E.
127–Linton, Ms Gwendolyn
128–Liverpool, Dr. J. A.
129–Lovell, Alfred
130–Lowe, Mr. & Mrs.
131–Lusan. Ms Carmen I.
132–Lund, John R.
133–Logan, Mrs. M.
134–Myers, Roy
135–Murrell, Mr./Mrs. Kenneth
136–Munro, Norma C.
137–Mowatt, Ms Unice T.
138–Monteith, Ms Alvira E.
139–Mott-Trille, Frank
140–Mooney, Ms Donna J.
141–Mitchell, Ms Lena E. B.
142–Mayers, Ian A.
143–Martin, Ms Cyrelene
144–Martin, Ms Florette J.
145–Marshall, Ms Syringa
146–Manley, Ms Madge
147–Magnus, Ms Mavis
148–Magnus, Frank
149–McDonald, Rupert g.
150–McGarvey, Mr./Mrs. James
151–McKenzie, Cecil
152–McNeil, Mrs. Gladys B.
153–McPherson, Ms Gloria N.
154–McVanell, Ms Bette Ann
155–Nugent, Ms Beryl May
156–Nurse, Harold
157–Nelson, Ms Amy
158–Orr, Mr./Mrs. Colridge
159–Oates, Ferven A.
160–Palmer, ms Carolina
161–Payton, Ms Joyce
162–Payton, Vivian
163–Perry, Lloyd, QC
164–Phillips, Mr./Mrs. Bradley
165–Pinnock, Ms Jeanne A.
166–Pinney, Mrs. Marjorie T.
167–Powell, Ms Pamela
168–Pasternik, Frank
169–Ramsay, Ms Thelma
170–Reid, Ms Una
171–Reuben, Cyril C.
172–Rowe, Ms Mildred
173–Russell, Alex
174–Richards, Ms J. Y.
175–Richards, Mr./Mrs. Arnold
176–Ricketts, Esmond S.
177–Riddell, Mrs. K. D.
178–Ringuet, Antonio T.
179–Ross, Mrs. Elaine
180–Reynolds, Ms Norma J.
181–Robinson, Howard
182–Robinson, Ms Moira E.
183–Rosseau, Ms Jeannette E.
184–Salmon, Mr./Mrs. Kenneth
185–Satchel, Ms A.
186–Scott, Mrs. Rose Veronica
187–Schloss, Ms Barbara
188–Schroeder, Harris P.
189–Sharpe, Bernie J.
190–Shaw, Mr./Mrs. Oliver B.
191–Sheppard, Carlton O.
192–Sheard, Mrs. Alva
193–Shoucair, Rudolph M.
194–Simpson, Ms Edith
195–Simpson, Valentine
196–Smith, Edward
197–Smith, Richard (Dick)
198–Smith, Ms Kathlene
199–Spencer, Ms Vivienne P.
200–Stewart, Ms Estelle R.
201–Stern, Ms Lucille
202–Templeton, Jr., Lester
203–Tennyson, Mr./Mrs. Owen
204–Thomas, Edwin
205–Thomas, Mrs. Elsian E.
206–Thomas, James Vangel
207–Turner, Ms Erma
208–Thompson, Melbourne
209–Vanier, Ms Emily M.
210–Vaughn, Mr./Mrs. Hugh A.
211–Vermont, Ms Dorothy
212–Walcott, Fitzroy
213–Wallace, Frank
214–Walker, Ms Veta
215–Walker, Leroy Samuel
216–Walker, Ms Myrtle D.
217–Welds, Edmond L.
218–Wetli, Ms Iris
219–Whyte, Ms Phyllis
220–Wigston, William Arthur
221–Wilson, Ms Ena G.
222–Wilson, Ms Eloise E.
223–Winchester, Wilbert
224–Wismer, Mr./ Mrs. Ray R.
225–Williams, K. D.
226–Williams, Ms Constance J.
227–Williams, Ms Daphne E.
228–Williams Noel O.
229–Williams, Mr./Mrs. Roy G.
230–Williams, Linford W.
231–Williams, Don B.
232–Williams, Ms Sylven E.
233–Woolston, Robert W.
234–Wright, John S.
235–Young, Ms Myrtle A.
236–Nichols, Henry
237–Osbourne, Ms Madge

Appendix 6

Jamaican-Canadian Association Executive and Other Committee Members 1962-2012

1962-1966—Roy Williams, Bromley Armstrong, George King, Ira Dundas, Mavis Magnus, J. B. Campbell, Owen Tennyson, Phyllis Whyte, Vie Carter, E.S. Ricketts, Frank Magnus, Roy Heron **General Purposes** Committee—Bromley Armstrong, Thelma Brown, James Johnson, Claudine Lewis, Alex Russell, Claude Forrester, Vie King, S. Black, and Gene Richards. ***Social and Publicity Committee***—Owen Tennyson, Trevor Anderson, Roy Heron, Byron Carter, Catherine Williams, Amy Nelson, Violet Carter, Adlyn Douglas, Lorna Dalrymple, Odessa Armstrong, Kathleen Smith, Carmel Ferguson, Marlene, Jeanne Pinnock, Gatchair, Viviene Spencer. ***Education Committee***—Frank Magnus, Mrs. Dorell Callender, J.B. Campbell, Bradley Phillips, Neville Fletcher, Dr. D.L. Foster. ***Membership Committee***—E.S. Ricketts, D. Eubanks, H. Daley, E. Eubanks, P. Whyte. ***Building Committee***—Roy Heron, Hugh Daley, J.DeSantos, G. King, E. Smith, A. Hastings, A. Russell, R. Williams, B. Armstrong and J.B. Campbell (No other information was available.)

1966-1970—***Board of Directors***—***Mel*** Thompson, Bromley Armstrong, Headley Tulloch, Orville Green, Alvin Curling, Mr. Dobson, Al Stewart-Gaynor, Canute J, Cato, Alva Kelly, Karl R. Fuller, Miss Olivia Grange, Stan Grizzle, Miss Norma Reynolds, Miss Joyce Stewart, Alton Telfer. ***Social Committee***—A. Russell, E. Keene, U. Soares, P. Terroade, P. Powell, R. Walker, G. Hylton, V. Melbourne, Cislyn Wright, H. Willis, G. Walker, G. Bruce. ***Education Committee***—Karl Fuller, Adlyn Douglas, Amy Nelson, Barbara Palmer, Barbara Schloss, Kathleen Smith. ***General Purposes Committee***—A. Stewart-Gaynor, Miss Phyllis Whyte, Mrs. Amy McDonald, Mr. Dudley Laws, Mr. Alva Kelly. ***Building Committee***—Bromley Armstrong, Karl Fuller, Amy Nelson, Adlyn Douglas, Sylvan Williams. (No other information was available.)

1971-1972—Bromley Armstrong, Headley Tulloch, Connie Whittaker, Canute Cato, Gwen Wolfenden Gladstone Hylton, Jim Bennett, Val Armstrong, Effie Keene, Erma Collins, Hugh Evelyn, Al Stewart Gaynor, Lloyd White (No other information was available.)

1972-1975—Mel Thompson, Ms. A. Johnson, Leithan LaFayette, Hugh B. Fg. Evelyn, H. Tony Walker, Ms Pauline Pigott, Ronald King, Byron Carter (No other information was available.)

1975-1977—***Board of Directors***—Canute Cato, Neville Walters, Rupert James, Nehemiah Bailey, Lilly-Ann Hatchett, Stanley G. White, Abigail Hamilton, Effie Keene, Derick Anderson, Amy Nelson, Monica Marsh, Joe Cross, Eva Smith, Noel Brown, Headley Tulloch, Mrs. Bev Folkes, Vincent Conville, Mel Thompson. ***Social Committee***—Neville Walters, Donald Biggs, Fred Ellis, Elvis Burrows, Val Armstrong, Raphaelita Walker, Vie Carter, Miss I. Cole. ***Building Committee***—Joe Cross, Daphne Bailey, Joslyn Thompson, Tony Biggs, Austin Davey, Amy Nelson, Raphael Walters, Horatio Samuels, John Bernard ***Women's Auxiliary***—Veta Walker, Derrick Anderson, Val Armstrong, Elaine Harris, Gifford Walker, and Gladstone Hylton. (No other information was available.)

1977-1978—***Board of Directors***—Dr. Vincent D'Oyley, Vincent Conville, Eva Smith, Jean Gopie, Neville Morrison, Randy Atkins, Joe Cross, Miah Bailey, Neville Walters, Dr. S. Wilson., ***Auditors***—Frank Wallace, Rodcliffe Williams. ***Membership Committee***—Randy Atkins, Beverly Johnson, Carmen Jens, Ismay Murray, ***Education Committee***—Rev. Audley Reid, Mrs. Monica Marsh. ***Trustees***—B. Armstrong, Adrian Chance, Amy Nelson, Roy Williams, John Davis. (No other information was available.)

1978-1980—Jean Gammage, Carmen Jens, E. Townsend, Lillian Hatchett, N. Morrison, Joe Cross, Eva Smith, Keith Mills, Rev. Audley Reid, Murline McDonald, Mel Thompson, Leroy Brown, Elizabeth Plummer, Hugh Morris, N. L. Bailey, Keith Mills, Jeff Patterson, Vincent Conville. ***Auditors***—Frank Wallace, Byron Carter. Trustees—Rupert James, Keith Mills, and Alton Telfer. (No other information was available.)

1980-1981—Mel Thompson, Miah Bailey, Hugh Morris, Lily-Ann Hatchett, Frank Wallace, Joe Cross, Carmen Jens, Ruel Grey, Daphne Bailey, John Brooks, Jean Gopie, (No other information was available)

1981-1984—**Board of Directors**—Rupert James, Hugh Morris, Nehemiah Bailey, Alton Telfer, Carmen Jens, Ruel Grey, Joe Cross, Lily-Ann Hatchett, Frank Wallace, Daphne Bailey, Erma Collins Norma Thompson, Orville Green, Mrs. Othlyn Frankson., Roy Williams. **Membership Committee**—Daphne Bailey, Cecil Brooks, Raphaelita Walker, Juanita Thompson, Jean Dockery, Muriel Aramdelovich, Collis Rattray, Wesley Grant. Raphael Walters, Thelma Allwood, Juanita Thompson, John Brooks. **Social Committee**—Anthony Biggs, Donald Biggs, Joe Cross, Jean Dockery, Fred Ellis, Devon Murray, Alex Russell, Josh Thompson, Juanita Thompson, Mrs. R. Walker, N. Walters, P. Williamson, Byron Carter, Barry Morrison, Raphael Walters, Thelma Allwood, Winnie Green, Carmen Jens, Roy Williams. **Building Committee**—Alton Telfer, Amy Nelson, Daphne Massey, Gifford Walker, Roy Stewart, Othlyn Frankson, Keith Mills, Alex Russell, Juanita Thompson, Norma Robinson, Hermine Johnson, John Brooks, Vie Carter, Erma Collins. **Trustees**—Joe H. Cross, Byron Carter, Amy Nelson, Alex Russell, Neville Walters. **Auditors**—Byron Carter, Jeff Patterson, **General Purposes Committee**—Eva Smith, Bev Folkes, Michele Davis, Lance Williams, Karl Oliver, Yvonne Ellis, Desmond Shepperd, Dudley Campbell, Leroy Brown, Zenora Brown, Tom Rhoden, Mona Ruhmann, Gary Wright, Everton Cummings, Karl Fuller, Volney Campbell. (No other information was available,)

1984-1988—**Board of Directors**—Roy G. Williams, Herman Stewart, Hugh Morris, N. L. Bailey, Erma Collins, Byron Carter, Hermine Johnson, Phitsbert Dawes, Shiela Raymond, Hyacinth Wilson, Frank Wallace, Veronica Hislop, Hector Gray, Neville Walters, Fred Irving, Eva Smith, Selwyn Noel, Jean Gopie, Minette Reid, Grace Baugh, Wesley Grant, **Social Committee**—Alvin Knight, Sonia Griffiths, Cyndi Anderson, Sylvester Symmonds, Joslyn Thompson, Raphaelita Walker, Ronald Amiel, Osbourne Miller, Gladstone Hylton, Yasmin (Jean) Henry, Juanita Thompson, B. Carter, Devon Murray, H, Johnson, T. Biggs, D. Biggs, E. Lyons, F. Ellis, R. Walters,

D. Sinclair, H. Wilson, M. Gardener, S. Raymond, R. Wright, S. Harrison, W. Harding, N. Stevenson, R. James, W. Green, J. Dockery, **Membership Committee**—Marilyn Amiel, Sheila Raymond, Cecil Brooks, Dorothy Dodds, Lorna Plummer, Averil Mills, Violet Carter, Cleveland Dale, Osbourne Miller, Daphne Bailey, Grace Baugh, Fred Ellis, Othlyn Frankson, Lloyd Hemming, Gladstone Hylton, Noel Maylor, Amy Nelson, Heather Rowe, Raphael Walters, Pearl Williams, Danny Donaldson, Joe Cross. Hugh Lawson, Jean Henry. **Building Committee**—Alton Telfer, Hector Gray, Herman Stewart, Collis Rattray, Miah Bailey, Alex Russell, Hermine Johnson, Keith Mills, Gifford Walker, Juanita Thompson, Roy Stewart, Neville Morrison. **General Purposes Committee**—Herman Stewart, Garth Christian, Roy B. Stewart, Mirabelle Corcho, Victoria Nelson, Ceceline Green, Zenova Brown, Coral Allan, Jerome Whyte. Desna Irving, Miah Bailey, Lloyd Henry, Roy Williams. **Fundraising Committee** Neville Walters, Theo Briscoe, Joyce Burpee, Karl Fuller, Winnifred Green, Carmen Jens, Paul Kafele, Amy Nelson, Sheila Raymond, Alton Telfer. **Womens' Committee**—Eva Smith, Theo Briscoe, Eunice Graham, Lorna Muir. **Trustees**—Theo Briscoe, Amy Nelson, Gifford Walker, Neville Walters, Alton Telfer. (No other information was available.)

1989-1992—**Board of Directors**—Miah Bailey, Frank Wallace, Byron Carter, Veronica Hislop, Hyacinth Wilson, Herman Stewart, Hector Gray, Sheila Raymond, Fred Irving, Karl Fuller, Cynthia Anderson, Elaine Thompson, Victoria Nelson, Zenover Brown, Mel Thompson, Marblet James, Barbara Thomas, Norma Larro, Any Nelson, Thelma Carey-Thompson, Austin Davey, Milton Pusey, Winnie Green, and Daphne Bailey. **General Purposes Committee**—V. Nelson, B. Walton, S. Harrison, V. Hislop, Roy B.A. Stewart. **Women's Committee**—Eva Smith, Theo Briscoe, Eunice Graham. **Building Committee**—Iris Henry, Herbert Green, Roy B. Stewart, Fay Conville, Vincent Conville, Gifford Walker, Eunice Graham, Ismay Murray, Marilyn Amiel, John Brooks, Keith Mills. **Trustees**—Theo Briscoe, John Brooks, Hermine Johnson, Alex Russell, Alton Telfer. (No other information was available.)

1992-1996—**Board of Directors**—Karl Fuller, Hyacinth Wilson, Cyndi Anderson, Fay Tallow, Bruce McDonald, Norma Larro, Erma

Collins, Jeff Patterson, Amy Nelson, Everton Cummings, Sandra Cornegie-Douglas, Herman Stewart, Marblet James, Miah Bailey, Lana Salmon, Anette Smith, Barbara Thomas, Daphne Bailey, Pam Powell. ***Social Committee***—Norma Larro, Junior Downer, Linda Gray, Pauline Reid, Lorna Salmon, Roy B. Stewart, Josh Thompson, Juanita Thompson. ***Building Committee***—Amy Nelson, Vincent Conville, Keith Mills, Herbert Green, Marilyn Amiel, Fay Conville, Eunice Graham, Ismay Murray, Junita Thompson, Iris Henry, Roy B. Stewart, Gifford Walker, John Brooks, Jeff Patterson, Marjorie Cameron, Trevor Lewis, Gladstone Hylton. ***Education Committee***—Erma Collins, Mary Barnswell, Theo Briscoe, Zenover Brown, Winnie Green, Rose Hodelin, Sam Otukol, Winnifred Plummer, Lorna Plummer, Billroy Powell, Herman Stewart, Syd Weir, Yasmin Aarons, Bunny Jackson, Elisha Steele. ***Trustees***—Alton Telfer, Hermine Johnson, Theo Briscoe, Alex Russell. (No other information was available.)

1996-2001—***Board of Directors***—Herman Stewart, Sandra Carnegie-Douglas, Alton Telfer, Cyndi Anderson, Vincent Conville, Fred Irving, Barbara Thomas, Pam Powell, Pat Williams, Pauline Tomlinson, Hector Gray, Francella Moore, Vincent Conville, Uriel Soares, Yvonne Wright, Elaine Thompson, Maxine Adams, Ruth Morris, Valarie Steele, Ansel Bather, Claudette Cameron-Stewart, Jaqueline Keene, Lana Salmon, Neville Walters, Zenover Brown, Dwight Barrett, Erma Collins, Lloyd Porter, Fay Conville, Teca Cameron, Barrington Morrison, Sydney Weir, Judith Spencer, Roy B. A. Stewart, Carlton Stewart, Sandra Stewart, Daphne Bailey, Vina Bennett, Leslie Small, Carl Lawrence, Hazel Small, B. B. (Barry) Coke, Anna Blakely, Donald O'Gilvie, Lloyd Porter, Una Smith, Clova Wolfe, Delores Lawrence, Ezra Nesbeth, Sandra Whiting, Baul Barnett, Leila McKenzie, Buddy McIntosh, Amy Nelson, Karen Smith, Patrick Chambers, Byron Carter, Linda Gray, Carol Plunkett, Gifford Walker, Dean Parker, Leon Sutherland, Adaoma Patterson, Rudolph McFarlane, Doug Robertson, Phyllis McFarlane, Victor Anderson, Ron Robinson, Louise Robinson, Owen Dunbar, Eric Malcolm, Carmen Sutherland, Herbert Green, Victor Anderson. (No other information was available.)

2002-2004—***Board of Directors***—Valarie Steele, Herman Stewart, Cyndi Anderson, Francella Vassell, Claudette Cameron-Stewart, Milton

Hart, Letna Allen-Rowe, Pamela Powell, Ruth Morris, Maxine Adams, Hector Gray, Michelle Blake, Leon Sutherland, Barrington Morrison, Pauline Reid, David Griffiths, Barbara Thomas, Patrick Chambers—**Building Committee**—Neville Graham, Dean Parker, Victor Anderson, Amy Nelson, Raphaelita Walker, Byron Carter, Owen Dunbar, Doug Robertson, Louise Robinson, Raphael Walters, Carmen Sutherland, Ron Robinson, Clive Hylton, Phyllis McFarlane, Eric Malcolm, Uriel Soares, Harold Green, Rudolph McFarlane, Gifford Walker, Maurice Wraith, Roy B. A. Stewart—***Seniors' Committee***—Ruth Morris—***Fund Raising Committee***—Daphne Bailey, Madge Cameron, Vincent Conville, Fay Conville, Lettice Davis, Bruce McDonald, Nola Moore, Hermine Johnson, Linda Gray, Herlinda Salmon, Hyacinth Wilson, Gale Henry, David Sinclair, Frank Wallace, Desna Irving, Sadie Harrison, Amy Nelson—***Golf Committee***—Erma Collins, Karl Killinbeck, Keith Mills, Alvin French, Earl Lalor, Winston Earle, Ivor Harriott, Alton Telfer Neville Miles, Jeff Patterson—***Nominating Committee***—Vie Carter, Byron Cater, Fred Irving, Sheila Raymond, Fay Conville, Vincent Conville—***North York Seniors Health Centre***—D. Bailey, A. Nelson, L. Gray—***Womens' Committee***—Marilyn Amiel, Zenover Brown, Norma Clarke, Ena Harrison, Ismay Murray, Lorna Plummer, Herlinda Robinson, Daphne Bailey, Theo Briscoe, Eunice Graham, Desna Irving, Rita McLean, Pam Powell, Carmen Sutherland, Bernice Bailey, Marjorie Cameron, Sandra Carnegie-Douglas, Esther Marks, Amy Nelson, Sheila Raymond, Raphaelita Walker—***Christmas Grand Market***—Alton Telfer, Hyacinth Wilson, Austin Davey, Norma Larro, Bruce McDonald, Maisie Allen, Hector A. Gray, Gifford Walker. (No other information was available.)

2004-2005—**Board of Directors**—David Griffiths, Herman Stewart, Cyndi Anderson, Desrene Lewis, Candace Earle, Sylvanus Thompson, Gary Thompson, LaToya McPherson, Julian Gordon, Leon Sutherland, Pamela Powell, Milton Hart, Ruth Morris, Richard Banton—***Building Committee***—Victor Anderson, Byron Carter, Owen Dunbar, Neville Graham, Herbert Green, Clive Hylton, Noel Lewis, Rudolph McFarlane, Eric Malcolm, Amy Nelson, Dean Parker, Louise Robinson, Ron Robinson, Doug Robertson, Nancy Stewart, Carmen Sutherland, Leon Sutherland,

Gifford Walker, Raphaelita Walker, Cleveland White—**Womens' Committee**—Bernice Bailey, Daphne Bailey, Theo Briscoe, Zenover Brown, Marjorie Cameron, Norma Clarke, Ruby Collymore, Eunice Graham, Camille Hannays-King, Ena Harrison, Amy Henry, Desna Irving, Ismay Murray, Amy Nelson, Lorna Plummer, Pam Powell, Sheila Raymond, Herlinda Salmon, Carmen Sutherland, Raphaelita Walker—**Education and Cultural Committee**—Joe Boateng, Fay Conville, Vincent Conville, Chantal Garnett, Daniel Hamilton, Judith Spencer, Ian Stephenson, Sylvanus Thompson—**Spelling Bee of Canada Planning Committee**—Natalie Blake, Natasha Blake, Joe Boateng, Ian Edwards, Lucretia Fletcher, Chantall Garnett, Rochelle Godfrey, Anneisha McLean, Dwaine Osbourne, Sylvanus Thompson—**Youth Committee**—Rachelle Alincy, Orville Anderson, Jacqueline Blake, Natasha Blake, Garnett Beale, Lisa brown, Latoya Christian, Andrew Martin, Rayon Maxwell, LaToya McPherson, Dainain Miles, Judy Morant, Dwaine Osbourne, Laurencia Paul, Max Pierre-Jermone, Roger Duffus, Samantha Ellis, Lurcretia Fletcher, Danielle Francis, Lorraine Reid, Nancy Stewart, Rowan Toban, Gareth Townshend—**Membership Committee**—Rachelle Alincy, Winston Brown, Hyacinth Cotrel, Myrtle Grant, Eulin Lewinson, Shirley McCoy, Dean Parker, Ina Powell, Pansy Stewart, Gary Thompson—**Fundraising Committee**—Daphne Bailey, Calvin Baker, Andrea Steward-Briggs, Marjorie Campbell, Lettice Davis, Marione Gardener, Millie Gordon, Linda Gray, Amy Nelson, Gary Nelson, Sandra Slyburne, Barbara Thomas Gifford Walker, Raphaelita Walker, Sharon Wynter—**Golf Committee**—Erma Collins, Winston Earle, Alvin French, Karl Killingbeck, Nevile Miles, Keith Mills, Adoama Patterson, Alton Telfer, Jeff Patterson—**Nominating Committee**—Marforie Cameron, Carol Plunkett-Fox, Dean Parker, Bruce McDonald, Monica Mitchell—**Seniors' Executive Board**—Luther Hayle, Iris Henry, Iris John, Yvonne Laing, Ruth Morris, Amy Nelson, Ron Robinson, Eula Smith, Lydia Thompson **North York Seniors' Health Centre JCA Representatives**—Daphne Bailey, Amy Nelson, Linda Grant. (No other information was available.)

2005-2008—**Board of Directors**—Sandra Carnegie-Douglas, Audrey Campbell, Billroy Powell, Nola Harris-Moore, Laurel Service, Dwaine Osbourne, Edna Smith-Bowes, Charmaine Sewell, Keith

Haye, Norma Brown-Larro, Sylvanus Thompson, Pam Reynolds, Rosemarie Powell, Barbara Thomas, Cynthia Anderson, Richard Banton, Leo Campbell, Luther Hayle, Camille Hannays-King, La Toya McPherson, Amy Nelson, Anton Squire, **Membership Committee**—Zenover Brown, Winston Brown, Covelyn Brown, Edna Smith-Bowes, Audrey Campbell, Pauline Reid-Douglas, Myrtle Grant, Enid Gough, Hector Gray, Keith Haye, Ina Powell, Eulin Lewinson, Shirley McKoy, Dean Parker, Rachelle Allincy, Pansy Stewart, Pam Reynolds, Lisa Marshall, Len Moore, Dwight Gordon, Shirley McKoy, Leo Campbell, Norma Brown-Larro—**Education Committee**—Vincent Conville, Fay Conville, Heather Robinson, Judith Spencer, David Allen, Dan Hamilton, Karen Tull, Chantal Garnett, Joe Boateng, Pam Reynolds, Sylvanus Thompson, Kellie Spence, Ian Edwards, Tamara Gordon, Roseanne Henlon, Julie Spence—**Fundraising Committee**—Daphne Bailey, Calvin Baker, Carlton Baker, Andrea Stewart-Briggs, Marjorie Campbell, Lettice Davis, Marione Gardener, Millie Gordon, Linda Gray, Amy Nelson, Gary Nelson, Sandra Slyburne, Barbara Thomas, Gifford Walker, Raphelita Walker, Sharon Wynter, Edna Smith-Bowes, Linda Gray, Bruce McDonald, Carol Fox, Rudolph Gibbs—**Building Committee**—Victor Anderson, Melody Brown, Byron Carter, Owen Dunbar, Neville Graham, Herbert Green, Clive Hylton, Noel Lewis, Rudolph McFarlane, Eric Malcolm, Amy Nelson, Dean Parker, Louise Robinson, Ron Robinson, Doug Robertson, Nancy Stewart, Carmen Sutherland, Leon Sutherland, Gifford Walker, Raphaelita Walker, Cleveland White, Keith Haye, Harold Goldson, Dwight Gordon, Rudolph Gibbs, Fitzgerald Davis, Patrick Moore, Everton Campbell, Chris Grant—**Youth Committee**—Rachelle Alincy, Lis brown, Danielle Francis, Roger Duffus, Samantha Ellis, Lucretia Fletcher, Elizabeth Huggins, Jacqueline Blake, Allison Johnson, Ashtona Johnson, Latoya Christian, Dainain Mile, Orville Anderson, Dwaine Osbourne, Laurencia Paul, Nancy Stewart, Rowan Toban, Latoya Wallace, Cassandra Walters, Antoinette Lewis—**Public Relations Committee**—Eunice Graham, Carol Plunkett-Fox, Claudette Cameron-Stewart, Avril James, Buelah Campbell, Natasha Blake, Milton Thompson, Baswell Wright, Melody Brown, Sheila Murray, Ann-Marie Whyte, LaToya McPherson, Norma Brown-Larro. Rosemary Powell—**Womens' Committee**—Bernice Bailey, Daphne Bailey, Theo Briscoe, Zenover

Brown, Marjorie Cameron, Norma Clarke, Ruby Collymore, Eunice Graham, Camille Hannays-King, Ena Harrison, Amy Henry, Desna Irving, Ismay Murray, Amy Nelson, Lorna Plummer, Pam Powell, Sheila Raymond, Herlinda Salmon, Carmen Sutherland, Raphaelita Walker, Charmaine Sewell, Rosemarie Hylton—**North York Seniors Advisory Committee**—Daphne Bailey, Amy Nelson, Linda Gray—**Golf Committee**—Keith Mills, Alton Telfer, Alvin Ffrench, Jeffery Patterson, Erma Collins, Adaoma Patterson, Winston Earle, Janet Neilson, Basil Daley Earl Sylvan Lalor, Cindi Anderson, Karen Tull—**Ad-Hoc Renovations Committee**—Billroy Powell, Charmaine Sewell, Keith Haye, Dean Parker, Audrey Campbell, Leon Sutherland. (No other information was available.)

2009-2009—Herman Stewart, Audrey Campbell, Solomon Spencer, Nola Harris-Moore, Norma Brown-Larro, Kelli Spence, Owen Dunbar, Dr. Sylvanus Thompson, Dwaine Osbourne, Pam Reynolds, Rosemarie Powell, Charmaine Sewell, Sandra Carnegie-Douglas. (No other information was available.)

2009-2012—Audrey Campbell, Carol Fox, Kellie Spence, Owen Dunbar, Sylvanus Thompson, Edna Smith-Bowes, Pam Reynolds, Rosemarie Powell, Charmaine Sewell, Dwaine Osbourne, Leo Campbell, Adaoma Patterson, Janet Samms, Herman Stewart, Ken James, Del Miller, Marcia Brown, Yolan Williams—**Building Committee**—Leon Sutherland, Amy Nelson, Herbert Green, Rudolph Gibbs, Dwight Gordon, Noel Lewis, Dean Parker, Doug Robertson, Gifford Walker, Clive Hylton, Rudolph McFarlane, Miah Bailey, Simone Banton—**Membership Committee**—Dean Parker, Dwight Gordon, Shirley McKoy, Pansy Stewart, Winston Brown, Eulin Lewinson, Coverlin Brown, Lisa Marshall, Len Moore, Pauline Reid-Douglas, Myrtle Grant, Ina Powell, Violet Dennison, Courtney Harriott, Leo Campbell, Norma Bredwood, Leona Earlington, Joanna Gordon, Judith Mitchell, Janet Samms, Mary Green, Herbert Green, Sonya Morris, Glenford Gordon—**Womens' Committee**—Bernice Bailey, Daphne Bailey, Zenover Brown, Marjorie Cameron, Norma Clarke, Ruby Collymore, Eunice Graham, Camille Hannays-King, Ena Harrison, Amy Nelson, Amy Henry, Enid Collins, Ismay Murray, Rosemarie Hylton, Lorna Plummer Pamella Powell, Sheila Raymond, Herlinda Salmon, Kristy Salmon, Juliett Saunders,

Carmen Sutherland, Raphaelita Walker, Jameleia Williams, Norma Bredwood—***Education Committee***—Roseanne Henlon, Julie Spence, Ian Edwards, Basil Dunn, Edeva Smith, Kellie Spence, Judith Spencer, Fay Conville, Dr. Vincent Conville, Heather Robinson, Tamara Gordon, Grace Williams, Dan Hamilton, Enid Campbell, Dr. Sylvanus Thompson, Marcia Brown, Sonia Deacon, Marcia Deacon, Del Miller—***Fundraising Committee***—Gifford Walker, Raphaelita Walker, Rudolph Gibbs, Linda Grey, Bruce Mc Donald, Norma Bredwood, Phillip Mascoll, Jody-Ann Tam, Sonja Morris, Michael Williams—***Youth Committee***—Ainsley Miller, Antoinette Lewis, Suzette Williams, Danielle Francis, Khaleelah McKnight, Jacqueline Blake, Zabrina Babbington, Angela Thomas, Nicole Mendez, Rosemarie Powell, Trecia Lamey, Yanique Williams—***Public Relations Committee***—Lauren Powell, Ainsley Miller, Jenita Brown, Yolan Williams, Zenover Brown, Sophia Daley, Ian Edwards, Marcia Higgins, Rosemarie, Hylton, Troy Logan, Adler Jean-Baptiste, Dwaine Osbourne, Sheila Raymond, Pauline Reynolds, Pethalee Robinson, Herman Stewart, Alton Telfer, Clayton Thomas—***North York Seniors' Advisory Committee***—Daphne Bailey, Amy Nelson and Linda Gray. (No other information was available.)

Appendix 7

Presidents of the JCA (1962-2012)
(in chronological order)

1. Roy G. Williams—1962-1966
2. Melbourne W. Thompson—1966-1971
3. Bromley L. Armstrong—1971-1972
4. Melbourne W. Thompson—1972-1975
5. Canute J. Cato—1975-1977
6. Dr. Vincent D'Oyley—1977
7. Dr. Vincent Conville—1977-1978
8. Kamala-Jean Gopie—1978-1980
9. Melbourne W. Thompson—1980-1981
10. Rupert James—1981-1984
11. Roy G. Williams—1984-1989
12. Nehemiah N. Bailey—1989-1992
13. Karl R. Fuller—1992-1996
14. Herman Stewart—1996-2001
15. Valarie Steele—2001-2004
16. David Griffiths—2004-2005
17. Sandra Carnegie—2005-2008
18. Herman Stewart—2008
19. Audrey Campbell—2009-2012+

Executive Directors of the JCA 1988-2012
(in chronological order)

1. Karl Fuller—1985-1987
2. Paul Kwasi Kafele—1988-1989
3. Janet Neilson—1990-1992
4. Haari Abou Korrat—1994
5. Billroy Powell (Interim)—1995
6. Akwatu Khenti-1995-1996
7. Deborah Headley—1996—1997
8. Haari Abou Korrat—1998-1999
9. Elaine Thompson 2000-2001
10. Errol Bonner (Acting) 2001-2003
11. Pat Williams 2003-2004
12. Danny Anckle 2004
13. Melody Brown 2005-2006
14. Joe Boateng (Interim) 2007
15. Nzinga Walker (Interim) 2007-2008
16. Karen Brown (Interim) 2008-2009
17. Michael Foster, CEO 2009

Appendix 8

Profiles of the First Executive Committee Members

The first Executive Committee consisted of 10 members two of whom served only until the election was held in the spring of 1963 and did not seek re-election. J. B. Campbell and Violet Carter demitted office and were replaced by Frank Magnus and Roy Heron who could then be seen as the Second Executive Committee. I will therefore profile them in that order.

Roy Williams was the Association's first president. Roy had come to Canada in September, 1953 to do graduate work at the University of Toronto to obtain his Master's Degree in Commerce and, subsequently, another Master's Degree in Economics and working towards a Ph.D. degree. He had learned the printing trade in Jamaica and used it to finance his way through College in the United States and in Canada where he worked the night shift at the Globe and Mail. He left that job to become an instructor and later Professor at Ryerson Institute (later Ryerson University). Roy was married to Catherine, had four children, and at the time lived in Scarborough. He had no previous involvement in community activities. He brought organizational and management skills to the new organization.

Bromley Armstrong was the Association's vice-president. He chaired the General Purposes Committee which was primarily responsible for the advocacy portfolio. Bromley had a long tenure in Canada. Having come to Canada as early as 1947 he was exposed to and actually experienced racial discrimination in all its ugly phases. In a previous job as a factory worker in the foundry of Massey-Harris (the now defunct farm machinery and heavy equipment manufacturer) he discovered first hand who got the dirtiest jobs and who were least likely to be promoted. This drove him into the arms of the Labor movement where he learned the techniques and tactics for championing the causes of those who were oppressed and underrepresented. This also cemented his socialist political orientation. These early experiences made an indelible impression on him and shaped his entire orientation to the society and his indefatigable, life-long efforts fighting racism and inequity wherever it may be found. Bromley also was involved with many nascent community organizations. This background was a strength that he brought to the group and later to the Association. He also had strong opinions on certain issues which he vigorously promoted, held on to, and from which he seldom relented. He was quite forceful in presenting and defending his positions. This of course contributed to some conflicts, but his vision and his history was critical in focusing the young association around issues of advocacy and activism

George King was the Executive Secretary. George, like Bromley, came to Canada in 1947. He had previously served many years in the armed forces in Jamaica, rising to the rank of Staff Sgt. Major, before coming to Canada. In Canada he worked at Massey Ferguson then in the printing trade and later with the Canada Post Office. He lived on College Street with his wife, mother and other family members. Their house was a meeting place for our planning sessions on many occasions. He, like Bromley, was involved with other incipient community organizations. They were compatriots. George was very punctilious about records, protocol and parliamentary procedures. He helped to lay a good foundation around these matters.

Ira Dundas was the Treasurer. Ira was a middle-aged gentleman who worked at Toronto City Hall as an accountant. He had been established in Toronto for a while. He was a quiet man, almost taciturn, not given to much talk and noisy arguments. He came aboard quite reluctantly as he was not too disposed to sully his well cared reputation by being associated with this new, untried group, most of whose members he did not know. Because of this he made sure that anything with which he was associated was very much above board. He was Mr. Integrity. He made sure that every penny earned by the Association was accounted for and deposited in the bank. If you spent any money you better be sure you had the proper documentation. He was not inclined to give his stamp of approval to anything that had even a hint of risk. He was ultra conservative but you could be assured that the Association's money was safe and the books and records balanced—every time.

Mavis Magnus was the Recording Secretary. Mavis was young and attractive. She was a pleasant, fun-loving person. She lived in Scarborough with her brother's family. But when it came to professionalism, expertise, and efficiency there was none better. She gave many, many hours of dedicated and devoted service to the JCA often after she had already done a full day's work at the Canadian Broadcasting Company (CBC). The professionalism of her output gave the stamp of legitimacy to any correspondence that went forth from the JCA office.

J. B. Campbell was the Chairman of the Education and Scholarship Committee. He was known and always addressed as J.B. He had come to Canada at least two to three years prior to the founding of the Association and had established himself. He was a Laboratory Scientist who had advanced his education from Jamaica to advanced studies in Atlanta, Ga., and later at Columbia University in New York. He was employed in a senior position at Connaught Laboratories and he lived with his family in North York. J. B. also came aboard with some reluctance, not being sure that he wanted to cast his lot with this unknown and untried bunch. He was a thoughtful man who was not indulgent of loquacious arguments. He was a voice of rationality in the early decision making but did not seek to be re-elected.

Owen Tennyson was the Chairman of the Publicity and Social Committee. Owen had come to Canada a few years earlier and had established himself. He was employed with the Shipping Company in Halifax and Montreal before being transferred to Toronto. He was also involved in the import-export business. He was a jovial man, quite extroverted and a hard worker. He was admirably suited to the Social Committee portfolio. He knew his way around Toronto and kept in touch with our members as he and his committee arranged functions and activities to bring bonding and cohesiveness to the group.

Phyllis Whyte was a Member-at-Large which meant that she was not limited to any one specific function on the Executive. She could be involved in any and all committees and specifically she would keep her eyes and ears attuned to the members' concerns and ensure that members' views were espoused at the Executive Committee level. She was a registered nurse and came to Canada among the wave of nurses who migrated to Canada after the door was pushed open by the efforts of the Negro Citizenship Association. This was done in 1953 when after much effort and petitioning the first nurse (Beatrice Massop) from the Caribbean was admitted into Canada. Phyllis worked as a nurse at St. Michael's Hospital for her entire career. She was a person of quiet demeanor, not overly talkative, but one who gave wise consideration to issues being debated. She was a solid member and contributor to that first Executive Committee.

Violet Carter was a Member-at-Large. As described above the Member-at-Large was free to serve on any and all committees but her primary concern was to be sensitive to the needs and concerns of the members and to present these to the Executive Committee. Violet (usually called Vi) was a registered nurse and had migrated to Canada in the early 1960's. She worked for many years with the Victorian Order of Nurses and later at Scarborough General Hospital. She was demure, soft spoken, very concerned about others and their sensibilities, very courteous and cultured. Vi served on the first Executive Committee but did not seek re-election. For her time on the Executive and for all her years in the Association, her constant concern was for the well-being of others. She was a lifelong member of the Jamaican-Canadian Association until her death in 2005.

Esmund S. Ricketts was a Member-at-Large. He was a grizzled veteran of both World Wars. He had been in Canada it seems like forever. He had always maintained his relations with the military and played the clarinet as he marched briskly with various military bands keeping pace with his much younger colleagues. He moved all around Toronto by foot and by streetcar and seemed to know every black family then living in Toronto. He was a very progressive individual and advocated for the upliftment of all black people. He was an ardent supporter of Marcus Garvey and was a member of the United African Improvement Association and its associated credit union. He would promote these to every black person that he met. He became the catalyst for the celebration of Jamaica Independence and the subsequent formation of the Jamaican-Canadian Association. He was abundantly enthusiastic and very inspirational. Ricketts died two weeks before the opening of Jamaica House on May, 1971.

Frank E. Magnus was the second chairperson of the Education and Scholarship Committee. He replaced J. B. Campbell who chose not to seek reelection in 1963. Frank was an accountant who worked for a construction company. He had served in the Canadian military and had become a Canadian citizen. He had married Bromley Armstrong's sister, Monica. It was therefore fairly easy for Bromley to recruit his brother-in-law to join the association and to accept a position on its board. Frank was the urbane, dignified gentleman who always spoke perfect English. (He seemed to be not familiar with the Jamaican dialect. He certainly didn't speak it.) He was the epitome of dignity and class. He too insisted on utter probity in everything that was being done by the association. He was a stickler for elevating standards to become a high class organization.

Roy Heron was elected to the Executive Committee in February, 1963. He replaced Violet Carter on the Executive Committee. He was a cousin of Bromley Armstrong, and a Veteran of the Second World War. He was a self-employed electrician who obtained his certification in Michigan and found it difficult to obtain equitably treatment by the Local Electrician's Union thus his support for the CCF (later NDP). He had three daughters and lived in Scarborough. He was an action-oriented person, not given to much temporizing and not enamored by ephemeral goals. He was appointed first chairman of the Building Committee and promptly set about on a variety of fundraising activities.

JCA First Executive Members (1962)

Bromley Armstrong   Owen Tennyson (D)*   Mavis Magnus Armstrong

Phyllis White   Violet Carter (D)*   Ira Dundas (D)*

George King (D)*   *Roy G. Williams*   J.B. Campbell

(D) - Deceased   Esmund S. Ricketts (D)
                         (no photo available)".

Appendix 7
Table 4
JAMAICAN-CANADIAN ASSOCIATION FINANCIAL DATA 1974-2011

	1974	1975	1976	1977	1978	1979	1980	1981	1982	1983
INCOME	25,422	39,987	40,111	14,167	N\A	23,219	27,658	35,268	36,517	31,785
EXPENDITURES	15,701	38,087	37,742	22,399	N/A	16,452	17,669	36,689	33,811	32,923
EXCESS INOME	9,721	1,900	2,369	8,232	N/A	6,767	9,989	1,421	2,706	1,138
MEMBERS' EQUITY	28,057	28,633	23,310	16,811	N/A	10,371	17,138	25,706	22,955	21,820
TOTAL ASSETS	35,597	135,795	138,492	132,572	N/A	34,220	84,625	46,938	67,863	80,696
MEMBERSHIPS	557	925	868	810	N/A	787	852	1,054	1,353	1,714

	1984	1985	1986	1987	1988	1989	1990	1991	1992	1993
INCOME	22,467	130,242	169,916	275,364	193,435	211,127	185,909	727,878	937,592	1,481,368
EXPENDITURES	24,538	95,206	162,653	186,038	147,075	172,304	199,805	704,843	860,303	1,435,162
EXCESS INCOME	2,071	20,137	7,263	9,480	11,247	13,787	13,896	1,225	56,965	46,206
MEMBERS' EQUITY	19,747	215,643	222,906	241,920	253,167	267,842	255,484	286,994	349,909	396,868
TOTAL ASSETS	107,082	322,725	461,697	502,140	498,437	416,146	398,117	420,221	431,012	460,747
MEMBERSHIPS	1,668	1,517	2,835	4,075	5,277	4,417	4,430	3,483	3,593	5,840

	1994	1995	1996	1997	1998	1999	2000	2001	2002	2003
INCOME	N/A	1,332,513	1,301,805	746,591	720,759	882,838	1,092,433	1,066,817	1,006,095	1,093,042
EXPENDITURES	N/A	1,319,190	1,262,391	727,810	708,305	730,104	1,000,501	1,015,128	999,237	1,099,679
EXCESS INCOME	N/A	2,183	37,274	36,506	12,454	152,734	91,932	51,689	6,858	6,637
MEMBERS' EQUITY	N/A	435,102	556,664	593,170	605,624	758,358	850,118	901,807	908,665	902,028
TOTAL ASSETS	N/A	518,412	999,323	1,024,831	1,030,326	1,336,900	1,855,735	1,778,366	1,707,968	1,626,349
MEMBERSHIPS	N/A	3,539	3,705	4,180	5,545	6,903	8,250	8,005	8,331	5,055

	2004	2005	2006	2007	2008	2009	2010	2011	2012
INCOME	1,188,626	1,142,742	1,308,889	1,775,818	1,947,893	1,981,016	2,030,765	2,071,086	
EXPENDITURES	1,144,541	1,177,462	1,242,992	1,720,952	1,982,605	2,057,588	2,061,099	2,082,235	
EXCESS INCOME	44,085	34,720	65,897	54,866	34,712	76,572	30,834	11,149	
MEMBERS' EQUITY	946,113	911,393	977,290	1,032,156	997,444	920,872	890,038	878,889	
TOTAL ASSETS	1,625,542	1,621,942	1,812,869	1,909,839	1,880,943	1,765,379	1,515,082	1,599,698	
MEMBERSHIPS	9,160	7,465	5,410	5,191	6,035	5,881	6,495	6,260	

Bibliography

Armstrong, Bromley L. *Bromley, Tireless Champion For Just Causes.* Pickering, Ontario:
Vitabu Publishing, 2000.

Grizzle, Stanley G, *My Name Is Not George: The Story of the Brotherhood of Sleeping Car Porters in*
Canada, Toronto, Umbrella Press, 1998.

Hill, Donna, *A. Black Man's Toronto*, 1914-1980, Toronto, Multicultural History Society of Ontario, 1981.

Hill, Dan, *I Am My Fathers' Son*, Toronto, Harper-Collins, 2010.

Manning, William, *My Name Is Eva*, Toronto, Natural Heritage/Natural History Inc., 1995.

Moore Donald, *Don Moore, An Autobiography*, Toronto, Williams-Wallace Publishers, 1985.

Walker, James W. St. G., *The West Indians in Canada,* Ottawa, The Canadian Historical Association, 1984.

Polyphony, The Bulletin of the Multicultural History Society of Ontario, *Toronto's People*, Vol.6 No. 1,
Toronto, Multicultural History Society of Ontario, 1984.

Toronto Mosaic 1988, A Conference on the Contributions of Immigrants and Refugees, Toronto, Toronto Mayor's Committee on Community and Race Relations, 1988.

A Minority Report, Toronto, The Toronto Star, 1985.

Edwards Brothers, Inc.
Thorofare, NJ USA
March 22, 2012